KATE MULVANY OAM is an award-winning playwright, screenwriter and actor. Her epic adaptation of the Ruth Park trilogy *The Harp in the South* played to great acclaim for the Sydney Theatre Company in 2018, and she followed this with her adaptation of Schiller's *Mary Stuart* for the company in 2019. Her play *The Rasputin Affair* was produced at the Ensemble Theatre and her play *Jasper Jones*, an adaptation of Craig Silvey's novel, has enjoyed great success at Belvoir Street Theatre, MTC, QTC and State Theatre Company of South Australia after its Barking Gecko premiere in 2015. In 2015 Mulvany's play *Masquerade*, a reimagining of the much-loved children's book by Kit Williams, was performed at the 2015 Sydney Festival and the State Theatre Company of South Australia as well as Melbourne Festival, produced by Griffin Theatre Company. Her autobiographical play *The Seed* (Belvoir Street Theatre) won the Sydney Theatre Award for Best Independent Production. With Mulvany performing in the play, it received great critical success and toured nationally, and is currently being developed into a work for screen. Mulvany's *Medea*, co-written with Anne-Louise Sarks, having been produced by Belvoir Street Theatre in 2012, won several awards including an AWGIE Award and five Sydney Theatre Awards, and has gone on to be produced in Poland, Basel, Auckland and at the Gate Theatre in London, to rave reviews. Other plays and musicals include *The Danger Age*, *Blood and Bone*, *The Web*, the musical *Somewhere* (music by Tim Minchin) and *Storytime*, which won Mulvany the 2004 Philip Parsons Award. As a screenwriter, she has worked on several television series, including *Beat Bugs* (the Emmy-award-winning series for Netflix) and the critically acclaimed *Upright* for Lingo Pictures. She is also an award-winning stage and screen actor with credits with many Australian theatre companies, television series and films. Most recently she played the eponymous role in *Richard III* (Bell Shakespeare) to great critical and popular acclaim, the one-person play *Every Brilliant Thing* (Belvoir Theatre) and can be seen as Sister Harriet in the acclaimed Amazon Prime series *Hunters*.

MARY STUART

an adaptation by

KATE MULVANY

after Friedrich Schiller

CURRENCY PRESS
The performing arts publisher

CURRENCY PLAYS

First published in 2020
by Currency Press Pty Ltd,
PO Box 2287, Strawberry Hills, NSW, 2012, Australia
enquiries@currency.com.au
www.currency.com.au

Typeset by Dean Nottle for Currency Press.
Cover design by Lisa White.
Cover features Helen Thomson and Caroline Brazier in the Sydney Theatre Company production. Photo by Brett Boardman.

A catalogue record for this book is available from the National Library of Australia

Contents

Currency Press acknowledges the Traditional Owners of the Country on which we live and work. We pay our respects to all Aboriginal and Torres Strait Islander Elders, past and present.

INTRODUCTION

The last decade at Griffin Theatre Company has given me the experience of writing about a play before I have made it. Currency Press publishes the new Australian plays produced there to be available in time for the first preview. This means the notes I am used to writing are still swimming in the unknown, the undetailed and the under-realised moments of week one or two of rehearsal. This is one of the first times I have been able to write about a play after the production … it feels great.

While there is so much to write about this production, I realise I am always drawn back to the mystery inside the moment I say yes to a play as a director, knowing full well that I am committing a chunk of my life to the creation and that I can never properly anticipate what it will cost me to make. There is, for me, a tipping point inside a script where I go from considering the possibility to knowing I will be doing it. In *Mary Stuart*, the scene that made the decision for me was the conversation between Elizabeth and Mary that is the climax of Act Three.

This is the first time a female playwright had been given the opportunity to write the scene between two of the most significant female figures of power in Anglo history for a mainstage production. So many men have had a crack at adapting the Schiller play. And I hadn't really been interested by any of them. Something inside this scene was something I had not heard before: a complex negotiation of ambition and privilege between two women of power with vastly different life experience, honeyed with all the humour, fatigue and compromise that belongs only in female conversation. I could feel Kate excavating a space no other woman has been allowed to in that prominent a place. It was significant for me that this play was going on the Roslyn Packer stage at Sydney Theatre Company. In the heart of theatre power in this country, a female voice was being given a platform, and in this scene she was taking the opportunity to speak. I was honour bound to say yes.

From the moment of our first reading I knew the whole play had to bend around making that scene work. Those 23 minutes were the heart of the play. It is written by a playwright who is also known to be one of our great actors. She could play either part, but that is not what you hear inside those lines—you don't hear an actor straining to be on the stage. You do hear a playwright who knows the actors who will play the roles intimately. You can hear her pushing them, offering them challenges, tempting them to use all their intelligence. There is so much scope inside these lines as an actor if you are smart enough to hear it. From the first read, both Helen Thomson and Caroline Brazier lit up with the potential they saw sitting on the page in front of them.

I learned an enormous amount about male power in the theatre while rehearsing this scene. All the women working in the room had been successful within the male structures of the Australian theatre world. And yet all of us had to learn to take the time and resources we needed and wanted to build the scene. It became apparent how well trained we all were to not 'waste anyone else's time' when we were working through difficult moments on the floor. We were all used to doing most of our work away from the room so as not to be the cause of a schedule overrun. None of us was comfortable keeping the 'men of the court' waiting for their next scene. That was never put upon us by the male cast members, it was something we put upon ourselves. This seems a small observation. That it was a revelation speaks to the rareness of the experience.

I look forward to this experience playing out across the country and over the years as the investment in this Australian adaptation of Schiller's play pays off. We will see what it means for the country to have a telling of this story in a distinctively Australian voice, rather than in the foreign tones of our colonial overseers. And I genuinely hope that this publication serves as a provocation to other commissioning companies around the world to ensure female playwrights are given opportunities to rewrite our imagined histories.

Lee Lewis

Lee Lewis is the Artistic Director of Queensland Theatre Company and former Artistic Director of Griffin Theatre.

AUTHOR'S NOTE

It was all about the 'echo' for me.

A seemingly obscure little breadcrumb hidden away within jumbles of research material as I set about writing this adaptation of *Mary Stuart* for the Sydney Theatre Company.

Until stumbling upon the 'echo', I'd found writing this piece a slightly frustrating process. Friedrich Schiller's 1800 original is a glorious work, structurally sturdy and poetically beautiful, but it still seemed to be missing something vital—an authentic female voice. I was surprised, too, that every adaptation of Schiller's play that I could subsequently find—and I searched high and low and wide and deep—had also apparently been written by men. Every one of these versions was unique and muscular and clever and powerful, but as a female adaptor, I suddenly felt the full weight of responsibility for these women and their legacies.

I decided to keep the structure of Schiller's original text—five acts, with the third act being a famously 'imagined' meeting between Elizabeth and Mary. I decided to branch out further than just the text on Schiller's page. I decided to start from absolute scratch to find out everything I possibly could about these Queens. I wanted to bring herstory to history.

I delved into the lives of Elizabeth and Mary and discovered details that intrigued and delighted me. 'Mary had a female jester'; 'Elizabeth was a keen matchmaker'; 'Mary enjoyed dressing as a man'; 'Elizabeth often dressed in a nun's habit'... My skin prickled with fury and sadness as I waded even deeper into the male-dominated worlds of these two women. 'When Mary was crowned at nine months of age, three men held her tiny body'. 'When Elizabeth was an early teen, she was likely sexually abused at the hands of a stepfather. When he was caught, it was Elizabeth who was asked to leave the house.' Mary was 'ground into the dirt', quite literally sometimes, by lovers and husbands alike. Elizabeth was 'constantly terrified of invasion, geographically and physically'— one of the reasons she never travelled and kept her court so close, like a barrier.

By the time Elizabeth was crowned at 25, she had experienced her father having her mother beheaded, had another stepmother die in childbirth, have another cast aside for being 'ugly', the next executed for adultery. By the time Mary's crown was lost, she had been raped, beaten, kidnapped, tortured and shamed. 'Burn the whore', the Edinburgh crowd screamed as Mary stumbled past them, beaten and betrayed, heavily pregnant with twins ...

She miscarried both.

What does this do to a woman? What effect do these sorts of events have on a mind and a body? Even in times of extreme brutality, they are horrifying histories. I felt I could hear Mary screaming across the Queendom to her 'High and Mighty Prince, sister and cousin, *ma chère amie*' to hear her—to honour her life the way that no man ever could. I felt I could see Elizabeth sit up on her throne and listen to her cousin's cry rolling across the land ...

And in this call is where the echo formed.

Whilst exploring the words and worlds of Elizabeth and Mary, I came across an intriguing chestnut. After Queen Elizabeth had had a particularly rough few months, and with her popularity at an all-time low, her long-time suitor Robert Dudley threw the Queen the 'greatest party of all time' and gave her a unique gift—an echo. Whatever the Queen uttered at the party—'Bring me more wine'; 'Another song, another dance!'—a voice, hidden amongst the guests, repeated the exact same words. When the Queen questioned who the anonymous parrot was, Lord Dudley replied, 'It is your gift. I give you your echo.'

Clever. After all, what do you give a woman who has everything?

Her own voice, apparently.

The Queen was said to be 'bemused'.

There was something about this 'echo', and the Queen's response, that resonated. That's what echoes do, after all.

My research took me into the story of Echo and Hera. As Dudley explains in this adaptation, Echo was a nymph who served Queen Hera. Echo was a delightful creature, but Hera noticed that people were listening to Echo more than they were to their own Queen. And so she silenced the nymph. She made it that Echo could only repeat what others had said.

This echo story encapsulated for me the psychological struggle between Elizabeth and Mary, but on an even larger scale, the way women are perceived in this world and pitted against one another. It is an ancient echo that says there is barely enough room for one woman of power in this world, let alone two. An echo that states in lurid print across trashy publications that any two royal women—be they Elizabeth and Mary, Margaret and Elizabeth or Diana and Sarah, or Kate and Meghan—will always be 'at war with one another'. An echo that says that any woman in power is really just a pawn moved around by men in the shadows. An echo that labels women as either 'virgin' or 'whore'. An echo that sees a 200-year-old play about two women only ever being adapted by men.

And so an 'echo' became the centrepiece for this adaptation—an *'idée fixe'* that reverberates throughout. It culminates in Act Three, when I decided to do away with Schiller's meddling menfolk altogether and have Mary actually become Elizabeth's echo … until she breaks Hera's ancient spell and the two start to properly converse, face to face for the first time. I wanted to sit these two Queens down, have them kick off their shoes, loosen their corsets, drink some wine, have a laugh and talk. Really talk. I wanted to explore the possibility that amidst the masculine maelstrom that surrounded them their entire lives, they loved one another, respected one another, yearned for one another. I wanted to show that these two women could very well be the best of friends.

It was important to me that I didn't portray Elizabeth I and Mary Stuart as pawns in a patriarchal chess game. They deserve better. In this adaptation, our Queens are the chess masters. They were taught the same false lesson we all were—'there is no room for two powerful women'—but in the spaces between history's dark truths, I wanted to explore the love, energy and friendship of these two incredible figures. Face to face. Woman to woman. Sister to sister. Allies. And yet walking hand in hand toward the heartbreaking inevitable.

I ached to change the ending, of course. That assaulting, real-life outcome was always a looming shadow over this work. Part of me still doesn't want to believe it really happened. Part of me wants to argue that in a game of chess the Queen has the power to move in any direction she likes. But this is not a game. And I couldn't change history, as much as I wanted to. So the inevitable had to happen, in all its brutal truth.

The wonderful director Lee Lewis urged me to inject a little hope, however. We decided to leave a resonating echo for the future—a positive one, this time—in the quiet presence of a Young Girl. Always onstage. Always watching. Always listening. The eyes and ears and voice of what is to come. She is our witness to herstory—an echo, calling across time to us all.

It was an honour to write this new adaptation, to meld my own female observations with Schiller's magnificent text. Yet much of what lays within these pages are the actual documented words of Elizabeth and Mary, in all their salty, sagacious and wicked wisdom. I hope you hear their words echoing in all the right ways, and that you enjoy getting to know them as much as I did.

Kate Mulvany
June 2020

The playwright acknowledges and gives thanks and respect to the Traditional Custodians of the land—the Gadigal People of the Eora Nation—on which this play was adapted and first performed.

Mary Stuart was first produced by Sydney Theatre Company at the Roslyn Packer Theatre, Sydney, on 9 February 2019, with the following cast:

MORTIMER	Fayssal Bazzi
MARY STUART	Caroline Brazier
PAULET	Simon Burke
SHREWSBURY	Peter Carroll
BURLEIGH	Tony Cogin
LEICESTER	Andrew McFarlane
DAVISON	Rahel Romahn
QUEEN ELIZABETH	Helen Thomson
AUBESPINE	Matthew Whittet
YOUNG GIRL	Darcey Wilson

Director, Lee Lewis
Set Designer, Elizabeth Gadsby
Costume Designer, Mel Page
Lighting Designer, Paul Jackson
Composer and Sound Designer, Max Lyandvert
Choreographer, John O'Connell
Fight Director, Nigel Poulton
Assistant Director, Madeleine Humphreys
Assistant Set Designer, Charles Davis
Voice and Text Coach, Charmian Gradwell
Production Manager, Genevieve Jones
Stage Manager, Minka Stevens

CHARACTERS

MARY STUART, an exiled queen

QUEEN ELIZABETH I, a reigning queen

AUBESPINE, the French ambassador

PAULET, Harry's jailer

MORTIMER, a soldier

BURLEIGH, High Treasurer

LEICESTER, Robert Dudley, Elizabeth's lover

SHREWSBURY, Elizabeth's counsellor

DAVISON, Elizabeth's secretary

EXECUTIONER

A YOUNG, NAMELESS GIRL

A SMALL DOG

SETTING

Mary's cell.

Elizabeth's court.

A garden party.

A scaffold gallows.

ACT ONE

SCENE ONE

Three huge crashes.

SCENE TWO: MARY

PAULET *and* MORTIMER *are in Mary's space beside a smashed harpsichord.*

MORTIMER *holds letters.*

MARY *strokes the dog on her lap.*

A nameless young GIRL *puts goods in a bag.*

PAULET: What is this …? What is this …?

    He finds letters.

  Mary, you continue to dismay me.

MARY: They're letters.

PAULET: Despite my supervision, despite my dutiful care, still you keep secrets from me?

MARY: They're just letters, Paulet.

PAULET: And in French, no less! Mary, Mary …

MARY: There's no sin in writing. It passes the time.

PAULET: Idle hours make for wicked thoughts.

MARY: Oh, Paulet, please.

PAULET: Who are they for? These enemy words?

MARY: They're private.

PAULET: Nothing is private in a prison.

    He reads them.

  Wait. Wait. Wait. This is the *Queen's* hand.

MARY: Yes. She wrote to me. Many times. Often in French.

PAULET: Since when?

MARY: Since she was a girl. Since we were girls.

PAULET: Why did I not know this? Why have you never shared these with me? Mary, Mary …

MARY: They're not for the eyes of men. They're women's thoughts. They'd be a foreign language to you, Paulet.

PAULET: I understand women. I understand women …

MARY: And how is Margaret?

PAULET: Furious as ever.

MARY: Send her my regards.

PAULET: I wouldn't dare.

MARY: And your daughters?

PAULET: God knows. They hardly speak to me. I may as well be invisible.

MARY: Well, you really should spend more time with them, Paulet.

PAULET: I know.

MARY: Go home to your wife and daughters. Let them tend to your ailment.

PAULET: Ha. Unlikely. They say I smell. Do I smell, Mary?

MARY: Not that I can discern, my friend.

PAULET: You don't find me pungent? I don't repulse you?

MARY: I've smelled much worse than a touch of gout in my life. Scotland, for example. Now go home.

PAULET: I can't just *go home*. You know that.

MARY: You need to rest.

PAULET: What if something happened here, Mary?

MARY: What could possibly happen within the confines of your inescapable oubliette, Paulet?

> PAULET *ruminates … then returns to the letters.*

PAULET: These will have to be confiscated and submitted.

MARY: Why?

PAULET: As further evidence.

MARY: Of what?

PAULET: Your … obsession with her. The Queen. Your infatuation.

MARY: *She* wrote to *me*, Paulet.

PAULET: This last one is dated quite some time ago … She lost interest, it seems. In you.

> *Beat.*

And what is this? Mary, what is this?

MARY: They're copies of my letters. To her.

PAULET: Your letters to … 'Queen Majesty', *'Ma chère amie Elizabeth …'*

'To the high and mighty *Prince* Bessie?!' Mary … everything you touch turns to menace.

[To MORTIMER]] Confiscate. Submit.

MARY: Please don't take them, Paulet. They're all I have of her anymore. Please, my friend. Don't.

PAULET *hesitates.*

MORTIMER *takes them from him and puts them in the bag.*

PAULET: They will be returned to you at a more … conscientious time.

MARY: All I request in those letters is her audience. To look her in the eye so that she may see I am not her enemy. I am her equal.

PAULET: No-one is Gloriana's equal, Mary.

MARY: She is the only person in this world that could possibly understand me and I am the only person in this world that could possibly understand her.

PAULET: Well, I like to think after all this time that I understand you, Mary. I understand you.

MARY: Of course you do, Paulet. You have been a great companion to me all these years. Poor Margaret.

She smiles at MORTIMER, *who continues to stare coldly.* PAULET *is mortified.*

But I do desire to speak with Gloriana as a sister, as a woman and as a queen.

PAULET: You are no longer a queen, Mary.

MARY: Well, you've made that clear. You've taken my rosary beads. My jewellery. My poetry. My music. My books. There's nothing else for you to take, unless you want to take the clothes off my back.

She smiles.

Would you like to take the clothes off my back?

PAULET: Contain yourself, Mary. Such goods only turn the heart to, to, to vanity, when it should be purging for atonement.

MARY: How can I atone for anything when you have taken my Bible?

PAULET: A sumptuously viceful life atones only through isolation and degradation.

MARY: Did you memorise that, Paulet?

He has no answer.

The tender errors of my youth shall be judged in the company of God and His saints. Soon, I expect. I am feeling quite weary.

PAULET: Are you? Shall I fetch you a cushion? Girl! Cushion!

The GIRL *hurries away.*

MARY: There is no mortal magister that can adjudicate me here.

PAULET: Well … you will be judged where you sinned, Mary. And that is in England.

MARY: But *what is* my sin? *What is* my crime?

PAULET: You know.

She stares at him blankly.

You're breaking the law right now.

There.

[*To* MORTIMER] See, Mortimer? Look at her. [*Calling to the* GIRL] Where is that cushion?

Look at you.

MARY: I'm just … sitting.

PAULET: But you're not, are you? You're doing so much more than that.

MARY: Am I?

PAULET: Yes! You're … you're …

Putting it out there.

MARY: Putting what out where?

PAULET: You're conspiring, even as we speak. I hear you whispering through the keyhole at night. I *hear* you, Mary.

MARY: [*whispering conspiratorially*] To whom am I whispering, Paulet?

PAULET: To, to everyone. Reaching through the lock like a, like a … Brandishing a, a, a torch of … civil war … You're … you're firing up the hearts and minds of the ordinary English.

MARY: Oh, is *that* what I'm doing? I had no idea.

PAULET: There's some say you are a *witch*. Do you know that?

MARY: Do they?

PAULET: I object, of course. I've seen no evidence of witchcraft since I've been your jailer.

Have I?

Mary?

Silence. He watches wide-eyed as MARY *raises her hands in a kind of spell.*

MARY: *Boo!*

>PAULET *shrieks in fright.* MARY *laughs.* PAULET *joins her.* MORTIMER *does not.*

Oh, Paulet, look. Ten fingers. No strange markings. Two nipples, last time I counted. But it has been a while since I've changed my underclothes. Would you like to prick me, Paulet? Just to be sure?

>*She smiles. He blushes.*

PAULET: Have you made pact with the devil, Mary?

MARY: Of course I have. I married him. Twice.

>*She laughs.* PAULET *can't help but join in.*

>MARY *winces suddenly.*

PAULET: Are you alright?

MARY: I'm fine.

PAULET: [*calling to the* GIRL] Cushion!

>*Beat.*

Of course, there are others out there that say you are a paragon of holiness. A saint.

MARY: Hardly. But I am a Catholic and I will serve no-one but God. As my husbands discovered.

PAULET: Mary. England's blood pit fills with hapless victims willing to sacrifice their lives for you.

MARY: Well, they shouldn't. I've done nothing to deserve their fervour.

>*She flares suddenly.*

God, *why* are we *still here*, Paulet? I arrived on this soil in need of assistance. Under threat of death. Assured that she—

PAULET: The Queen.

MARY: —would offer her bosom / to rest my head—

PAULET: Please don't speak of the Queen's / bosom.

MARY: —in full confidence that I would be welcomed into a sister's / embrace.

PAULET: Cousin.

MARY: Only to be locked away, in confinement, for nineteen years, under your bloodshot / eye.

PAULET: Because you are a criminal!

MARY: I am a hostage!

PAULET: You're a terrorist, Mary!

MARY: I am not, man.

> *Beat.*

I did not come to England to take the throne. I willingly abdicated my own throne. Why would I want another one?

PAULET: We need your signature.

MARY: You have my word.

PAULET: But we need your name, / Mary.

MARY: Paulet …

You have all of my earthly belongings in that bag of / yours—

PAULET: You still have the dog. /

MARY: —and yet here I am, offering you my most precious possession— my absolute word—and you won't take it. You have never taken it.

PAULET: It's not up to / me—

MARY: A piece of paper can be forged, torn, burned … But my word can't. My word is stronger than my scrawled name. So please. Take my word. Take it and put it in that bag with all my other goods.

Bring it here. Please, my friend.

> *She gestures for* PAULET *to bring the bag. He does, confused. She shouts into the bag.*

Hello! I come in peace! I do not want the English throne! I would simply like to meet my sister-cousin, the Queen! I have much to chat to her about!

> *She closes the bag.*

There. My word. Take it and share it with the 'magistrates'. All forty-two of them.

MORTIMER: You're not a queen. You're a whore.

> *Beat.* MARY *turns to* MORTIMER, *shocked.*

PAULET: Mortimer …

> MORTIMER *silences him.*

MORTIMER: A wanton bitch who married a sickly child to get a French crown on your head because your Scottish one was a shit-stained piece of tin, a gutless slut who had your second husband murdered, then took his killer as your third husband, a harlot on the run from your own people, exiled from a throne contaminated by your own filthy, adulterous ways, a hypocrite against your own God-awful Catholic faith. Even your looks have faded, probably through the guilt and treachery lurking beneath your yellow skin, you fucking. Scots. Frog.

Silence. MARY *stares at him, horrified.*

PAULET: Mortimer. We … we don't speak that way. Not in my prison. Letters.

He smiles apologetically at MARY *who is glaring at* MORTIMER.

Well …

MORTIMER *looks to the bag in his hands.*

Yes.

Watch her, Mortimer. Nicely.

MORTIMER: Yes, Uncle.

PAULET *goes to leave, then turns.*

PAULET: You don't realise how difficult it is to have this cursed authority, Mary. To know that one mistake from me could lead to the death of a queen.

Her.

Or you.

I don't sleep at night, for fear I've left your door unlocked. That I've let the enemy out. Or in. I check it every hour, obsessed. I tremble until morning. Night after night. Year after year. I quake.

It is no easy task being your jailer, Mary.

It is no easy task being the keeper of queens.

MARY: Well, you won't have to worry yourself much longer, Paulet. Soon you can return to your wife and daughters. Any will I might have once had has long vanished. I am mortally tired. May I request a priest to give me sacrament before I fall into eternal sleep?

Beat.

PAULET: I will see what I can do, Mary.

MARY: Thank you, my friend.

PAULET *leaves, holding her letters.*

Silence.

Suddenly ...

MORTIMER *weeps.*

MARY *stares at him.*

What's wrong with you, man?

MORTIMER *is inconsolable. She watches.*

He finally regains his composure.

MORTIMER: I apologise for my language ... I beg forgiveness ...
I ...
I am your servant.

He falls at her feet.

Oh, Queen ...
I am Mortimer. I am new to this court, but I secretly share the same faith as you ...

He looks at her briefly.

Oh, Mary ... My Queen ...

He struggles to find his words.

I ... loathe the reformation of this country.
When I returned from war I hardly recognised my own homeland ...
God's vivid spirit has been deprived of my people. So I ran away to immerse myself in the Catholic realms abroad. To behold once more the spectacle of the Mass. The miracle of the Sacrament. Spain, Italy, your beloved France—I went to them all.

Silence. She stares at him. Then ...

MARY: Tell me more.

MORTIMER: I ... I joined passionate pilgrims on holy roads ... Like we were bound for Heaven itself ... In Rome, I saw the Pope in all his splendour—the conduit for the birth of the Lord, the Holy Mother, the descending Trinity, the luminous Transfiguration ...
I ...

He looks up at her awestruck.

Oh, Queen ...

I watched the Pope give the Mass in a church of glittering gold. Ceilings painted with vast images, windows of glass twinkling with icons. Music, song, verse, voices, filled the air like flights of angels …
I found myself brimming with … abundant love.

MARY: Goodness. How wonderful for you.

MORTIMER: And on my travels … I carried a picture of you with me. Look.

He shows her.

MARY: I barely remember that girl.

MORTIMER: You accompanied me to all of those sacred places, Queen. Like you were bearing witness alongside me.

MARY: But I wasn't. I was in here.

MORTIMER: I showed this picture to everyone I met. And everyone I met—the brothers, the bishops, even the *priests*—they fell in love. With your face and your faith.

MARY: Did they?

MORTIMER: Please, Queen Mary. Please let me prove to you my devotion.

He starts to undress.

MARY *stands, threatened.*

MARY: I'm warning you, I have killed far greater men than you.

MORTIMER: Please. Queen. I will not hurt you. Look.

His shirt is removed.

His torso is a mass of tattoos of Catholic icons.

And Mary's face.

Do you see? It's you. Your image. Carved forever over my beating heart.

MARY *reaches out to his skin. Runs her hand over the images, awestruck.*

He kneels before her.

Majesty …
There is an army of Catholic warriors the world over who have vowed to fight for you … French. Spanish. Italian. Scottish. Irish. English.
I carry the hearts of thousands upon thousands who demand your freedom. Their voices are getting stronger by the day. They know the

righteous pathway to the English throne has been wickedly deviated. That a bastard queen has stolen your seat. They will not rest until you wear the crown. I will not rest until you wear the crown. You are the one true Queen.

Mary Stuart.

One-time Queen of France.

One-time Queen of Scotland.

Rightful Queen of England.

MARY: You are mad.

MORTIMER: Mary, your incarceration has stolen your dignity. This dungeon has robbed you of your beauty, but you are still adorned with light and life. I see that. I feel that.

Silence.

MARY: So what do I do?

MORTIMER: My Queen?

MARY: Just sit here and twiddle my thumbs for another twenty years while you lot spend your days getting pretty pictures painted on your skin?

MORTIMER: We will get you out. You are our living saint. We all have your image etched across our hearts.

MARY: Oh, you men. Getting all primed and passionate over a twenty-year-old painting of me. Put your clothes on, for God's sake.

MORTIMER: Well, yes, / but—

MARY: It's ridiculous.

MORTIMER: Is / it?

MARY: And arrogant. Put your clothes on!

He dresses quickly.

MORTIMER: I don't mean to / offend—

MARY: This army of Catholic warriors you speak of … you don't think maybe I had something to do with that? That the blood in my veins has something to do with that? That my own courage and resilience and legacy might have something to do with that? That God might have something to do with that?

MORTIMER: Of course. God. Yes.

MARY: You're more than welcome to join our crusade. Mine and God's. But I'm not about to join you and your international band of inked zealots. Understand?

I am in poor health.

Even if they were to extend my sentence by a mere month, I doubt I'd see the end of it.

MORTIMER: Please stay strong, Queen. You have support. They are on their way. The men.

MARY: Please don't show my picture to any more men. I don't want them to be disappointed should they ever get here.

MORTIMER *hurries to his feet as* PAULET *enters with* BURLEIGH.

BURLEIGH: Mary Stuart.

MARY: Lord Burleigh.

BURLEIGH: The forty-two high judges have reached their verdict.

MARY: Oh. Has my sentence finally been pronounced?

BURLEIGH: You have been found guilty.

MARY: Of what crime?

BURLEIGH: Treason.

MARY: I am not a citizen of this country. Therefore a charge of treason is impossible.

BURLEIGH: You are guilty, woman, of conspiring to kill the Queen, citizen or not.

MARY: Which queen, man? Myself? Because I have contemplated that many times in my life.

BURLEIGH: Queen Elizabeth. Daughter of King Henry VIII. The Virgin Queen. Gloriana.

MARY: I conspired to kill all of them, did I? I have been busy.

BURLEIGH: You conspired to murder the Queen of England.

MARY: How did I manage that from in here? And at which point in the past two decades did I do such a thing? Please remind / me.

BURLEIGH: We found proof.

MARY: What proof, sir?

BURLEIGH: Letters conspiring to kill Gloriana. Written over the past year. With your signature on the bottom. We have confessions from your allies.

MARY: I wasn't aware I had any allies.

BURLEIGH: You don't. Not anymore. They have been disposed of.

Beat.

MARY: I shall pray for their innocent souls.

Paulet, have you ever seen a letter of conspiracy leave this room?

PAULET: I … The … the only letters I have ever seen are those I brought to you today, Lord Burleigh.

MARY: Yes. My private correspondence with Elizabeth.

BURLEIGH: Then, Paulet, you should have paid less attention to your prisoner's beguiling charms and more to her cunning wiles. The signature on both sets of letters—personal and treasonous—comes from the same hand. Mary Stuart's.

MARY: I want to see these letters of treason.

BURLEIGH: They have been confiscated. Submitted.

MARY: Show me the proof of my crime, Lord Burleigh.

BURLEIGH: Your *name* is the proof, Stuart. Your name is cutting a murderous swathe through this country. There's blood on the streets thanks to your malevolent Catholic enclaves breeding all over the place.

MARY: I have instigated no uprisings.

BURLEIGH: Then why the unrest?

MARY: Perhaps the English are deciding their own future?

BURLEIGH: No. The English don't do that.

MARY: All I have ever wanted is our two countries to live as peaceful neighbours. Safe and secure in each other's familial embrace. I deny any wrongdoing. I have urged no rebellions. I have been here alone for nineteen years.

PAULET: *I've* been here with you. And you have a dog. We gave her a dog.

MARY: I am no conspirator.

BURLEIGH: Tell that to your dead husbands.

> *Beat.*

MARY: It is prescribed by English law that every defendant shall be judged by a jury of equals. Who on that jury of men is my equal? Only kings are my equal.

BURLEIGH: You dare question forty-two high judges?

MARY: You dare question one queen?

BURLEIGH: Woman. Forty-two of the finest men in England served this trial. Noble governors of liberty and justice.

MARY: So I am being judged by the same men who have changed their convictions under four consecutive governments? Judged by men who alter their faith as rapidly / as the seasons?

PAULET: Mary. Contain / yourself.
BURLEIGH: Whilst you breathe the air of this country, / Stuart—
MARY: This cell.
BURLEIGH: —you *will* be judged by the great men of / this country—
MARY: Only God has the right to judge a / queen.
BURLEIGH: You will be judged by the great reformers / of this country,
    woman—
MARY: Reformers? Changing God's word to suit your own filthy /
    proclivities—
BURLEIGH: You will be judged by the great men, the reformers / of this
    country, Stuart—
MARY: The same great men who put the bastard daughter of a fat, stinking
    philanderer and a conniving whore on the throne?

> *Horrified silence.*

My apologies. My temper sometimes gets the better of me.
    I do not judge the Queen, nor her parents.
    It's just …
    I was hoping to go home.

> *The* GIRL *runs back on with a cushion.* PAULET *takes it, furious.*

So it seems I shall live out my life under your trembling eye, Paulet.
We're stuck with each other in this eternal dungeon. Your wife will
be furious. Poor Margaret.
BURLEIGH: Not necessarily. The sentence is still being decided.
MARY: Well, tell them to hurry up. I'm weary.
BURLEIGH: The decision rests with the Queen.
MARY: Elizabeth.
BURLEIGH: Gloriana.
PAULET: She's ruminating.
MARY: On what?
BURLEIGH: The law states: 'If a plot in the kingdom rises in the name
    of, and for the benefit of any person who pretends rights to the crown,
    one should go to court against them and until death the guilty one
    pursue'.

> *Beat.*

MARY: I do not know this law.
BURLEIGH: It's a new one.

Beat.

MARY: She would dare put a crowned head on the block?

BURLEIGH: There's been no crown on your head for two decades, Stuart.

MARY: Does she not fear the wrath of France?

BURLEIGH: The Queen and France have cultivated a newfound endearment. They are happy bedfellows. It seems you have been cuckqueaned.

MARY: What of the King of Spain? Will he raise his weapon in defence of me?

BURLEIGH: I suspect the Spanish are too busy licking their wounds after an English trouncing. You know what that feels like.

MARY: She would remove the head of a cousin? A sister?

PAULET: She has not decided yet, Mary. But she does have a heart of mercy.

BURLEIGH: This country has had its share of royal women descend the throne only to ascend the scaffold. You are not unique, Stuart.

> MARY *stares at him.*

MARY: *Pourquoi as-tu une telle soif de sang d'une femme, Monsieur Burleigh?*

> *Beat.*

BURLEIGH: You've long outgrown your exotic allure, Stuart. There's no sign of that sweet Parisian prettiness that once illuminated your face. Not even an endearing flush of salty Scottish passion. There's just … nothing.

How lucky for you there is no mirror in here.

> MARY *turns from him.*

MARY: May I receive a priest, now, please, Paulet?

BURLEIGH: We can provide a dean.

PAULET: I had promised her a / priest.

BURLEIGH: We can provide a dean.

MARY: I would like a Catholic priest to hear my final confession and provide the Sacrament, Lord Burleigh. I fear if I die soon, either in here or on the scaffold, my soul won't find its way to Heaven. [*To* PAULET] Please.

BURLEIGH: You can pray on your rosary beads, Stuart.

PAULET: We took them, Burleigh.

   BURLEIGH *takes them from the bag. They're gold.*

BURLEIGH: Aren't they pretty.

   He keeps them and goes to leave.

MARY: Lord Burleigh …

   He turns.

Has there been any word from my son?

BURLEIGH: The King of Scotland? Actually, yes. He sent a jewellery
   box.

MARY: For me?

BURLEIGH: For Gloriana.

   Beat.

MARY: Will I see her?

BURLEIGH: The Queen?

MARY: Yes.

BURLEIGH: No.

   The men leave.

   MARY *and* MORTIMER *share a glance as he exits.*

   MARY *composes herself. Just.*

   Goes to a secret hiding spot.

   Pulls out a piece of paper and starts writing.

END OF ACT ONE

ACT TWO: ELIZABETH

SCENE ONE

ELIZABETH, AUBESPINE, LEICESTER *and* SHREWSBURY, *who is covered in blood.*

The young GIRL *is there too.*

ELIZABETH: Are you *sure* there's nothing on me?

AUBESPINE: You are as perfect as ever, Your Highness.

ELIZABETH: Are you *sure* though? Take a good look.

> *She turns around before them.*

LEICESTER: You're as fresh as new snow, Bessie.

ELIZABETH: Oh, Shrewsbury. Look at you.

LEICESTER: You look a mess, Shrewsbury. An utter mess.

SHREWSBURY: That will be the blood, sir.

ELIZABETH: Came out of nowhere. Did you see it coming? I didn't see it coming.

AUBESPINE: It was quite a shock, Your Highness.

ELIZABETH: I mean, who throws a bucket of blood over an old man? Poor Shrewsbury.

SHREWSBURY: I don't think they were aiming for me, Your Majesty.

ELIZABETH: Wait, you don't think—

SHREWSBURY: I believe when the man cried, 'Die, Gloriana' as he threw the bucket of blood, he was probably referring to you rather than me, Your Majesty.

ELIZABETH: Oh, is that what he said? I couldn't hear for the noise. Such ruckus on the streets lately.

AUBESPINE: Thank God he was such a bad shot, Your Highness.

ELIZABETH: Why would he throw blood on me?

AUBESPINE: There is no blood on you, Your Majesty.

ELIZABETH: We live a very peaceful life in this country.

AUBESPINE: England is very serene, thanks to you, Your Majesty.

ELIZABETH: I don't like wars. They have uncertain outcomes. Are you *sure* there's none on me?

LEICESTER: You really shouldn't venture out so much, Bessie darling.

AUBESPINE: I agree, Monsieur Dudley.

ELIZABETH: *Leicester*. He is *Leicester.*

AUBESPINE: My apologies. Leicester.

LEICESTER: It's getting a little precarious out there, Bess.

ELIZABETH: Nonsense. They're my subjects. They deserve to glimpse their queen. They like it. It brightens their day. I wonder whose blood it is.

SHREWSBURY: So do I, Ma'am.

ELIZABETH: Probably a pig. Or a cow. Maybe a few dogs. Oh, I do hope this hasn't marred your view of our country, Ambassador Aubespine.

AUBESPINE: Oh-beh-peene. Not at all. / Not at all.

ELIZABETH: I would be simply mortified if you had to return to Paris and tell the Duke, 'I took a lovely trip up the Thames, dined at the palace, met the Queen's devoted subjects and then a madman threw a bucket of blood over one of her elderly servants'.

AUBESPINE: I'd already forgotten that part, / Your Highness.

ELIZABETH: I'd just hate for the Duke of Anjou to get the wrong idea about me. He's got enough to worry about. The poor little scoliotic frog.

AUBESPINE: Yes, well. It would be good to ascertain just what news I will be taking back to the Duke. He awaits your answer with great excitement.

ELIZABETH: Does he? Does he really?

AUBESPINE: Of course.

ELIZABETH: Even with all those French women around him? Those sexy, pouty, fashionable, miserable French women?

AUBESPINE: Even so.

ELIZABETH: He does like women, doesn't he? He's not like his brother, is he?

AUBESPINE: You mean the King of France, Your Majesty?

ELIZABETH: Mm. The King. I hear he wears gowns.

AUBESPINE: He has … endearing sartorial quirks, Majesty.

ELIZABETH: And he prefers the company of men?

AUBESPINE: It is a most masculine court, Majesty. Much like your own.

ELIZABETH: And he thinks I'm an old, decrepit wench who will probably die soon so he may as well betroth me to his bent-back'd brother to make the English throne French when I finally fall off my gilded perch.

Silence. The ambassador looks confused.

Or am I mistaken, Ambassador?

AUBESPINE: I can assure you, the King of France is a great admirer of yours.

ELIZABETH: And my closet, no doubt.

She laughs. Everyone follows suit.

AUBESPINE: And his brother the Duke of Anjou has only the highest of intentions for his beloved English queen. He loves you deeply.

ELIZABETH: And I love him. I do. It's just that I've come this far, Ambassador. After all, I am …

SHREWSBURY: Fifty-four.

ELIZABETH: A *virgin,* Shrewsbury. And I had every intention to die one. But although I have governed like a man and a king, my sex betrays me, I'm afraid. I may be queen, but I am still expected to 'obligate nature'. Submit to its terms. My people *insist* on an heir, you see, Ambassador. They want to see these features, inherited from my father—

SHREWSBURY: You actually look more like your mother.

ELIZABETH: —these features inherited from my father, the great King Henry VIII, my people want to see them passed on. And I understand that. I do.

LEICESTER: You can't have a child, Bessie. You're too … mature.

ELIZABETH: I am more than aware of my own body's capacities, Leicester. I'm perfectly capable of procreation.

AUBESPINE: Of course you are. And I'm sure your glorious attributes will unify beautifully with those of the Duke of Anjou.

ELIZABETH: The frog. Yes.

Beat.

Tell me, Ambassador. Does the pretty little King of France get as much pressure put on him to produce an heir by his court of men?

AUBESPINE: King Henry is a proclaimed bachelor.

ELIZABETH: Ah. Of course. Lucky him.

AUBESPINE: He leads a most extravagant and exciting court, Your Majesty. You will fit right in. We will dress you in the finest French fashions. The most famous French dramatists will write for you, perform for you. The most heartbreaking of tragedies.

ELIZABETH: Oh please, no.

AUBESPINE: Biblical tragedies.

ELIZABETH: No.

AUBESPINE: Ancient tragedies.

ELIZABETH: No.

AUBESPINE: Contemporary tragedies.

ELIZABETH: How morbid. No.

AUBESPINE: But we also have the finest of comedy!

ELIZABETH: Ugh …

AUBESPINE: We have tragicomedy!

ELIZABETH: No.

AUBESPINE: Pastoral comedy!

ELIZABETH: No.

AUBESPINE: Commedia dell'arte!

ELIZABETH: God, no.

AUBESPINE: Farce!

ELIZABETH: *No*, Ambassador! No! The French aren't funny.

AUBESPINE: Well … if quiet meditation is more to your liking, Your Majesty, we could find you a good tutor to perfect your French tongue.

Silence. She turns. Smiles at him.

ELIZABETH: How kind of you, Ambassador. Or should I say, *'C'est très aimable à vous, Ambassadeur'*.

AUBESPINE: Ah! You speak beautiful French.

ELIZABETH: *Oui. Je parle parfaitement Français.*

AUBESPINE *nods, humbled.*

Also …

Parlo Italiano perfetto.

He nods again. Ahh …

Also …

Hablo Español perfecto.

AUBESPINE *nods again. Ahh …*

Also …

Latine perfecta loquor, loqui.

Silence. Ahh ...

So I won't be needing a 'tutor' in any tongue, Ambassador Aubespine. *Merci beaucoup. Grazie. Gracias. Gratias tibi ago.*

An awkward silence.

AUBESPINE: So ...

ELIZABETH: Hm?

AUBESPINE: So may I tell the Duke ... your answer ... is an affirmative? That you will finally accept his marriage proposal?

ELIZABETH *sighs.*

ELIZABETH: The Queen has no more say in such things than a common woman does. The same signs signify the same service. So here.

She pulls a ring from her finger.

Give him this ring to commemorate the confidential circle of our nations' embrace.

He goes to take it. She pulls it away.

But if France seriously desires my alliance, it must also share my worries and not befriend my enemy. Yes?

AUBESPINE: But of course.

She gives AUBESPINE *the ring.*

So it is affirmed? It is affirmed?

ELIZABETH: Definitely.

AUBESPINE: Ah!

ELIZABETH: Definitely an affirmative maybe.

He is confused.

Lovely seeing you again, Ambassador. Till next time.
Au revoir.

An awkward beat.

AUBESPINE: Your Majesty.

AUBESPINE *leaves.*

ELIZABETH: For God's sake, Shrewsbury. Clean yourself up.

SHREWSBURY: Yes, Your Majesty.

ELIZABETH: [*to* LEICESTER] And what's wrong with you?

LEICESTER: What do you *think*?

ELIZABETH: Oh, Robert. It's politics. It doesn't mean anything.

LEICESTER: It does to me. You've never given me a ring.

ELIZABETH: It's a trinket. A trifle. It's important the French think they might win me. We have to let them believe they mean something in the grand scheme of things. We can't disrupt international relations for the sake of your bleeding heart.

My tooth hurts. Kiss it better.

She gives him a kiss.

Do I taste good?

LEICESTER: Always.

BURLEIGH *arrives, with* DAVISON.

BURLEIGH: Your Majesty, I just heard about the assassination attempt.

ELIZABETH: It wasn't an assassination attempt, Burleigh.

BURLEIGH: Were you there, Dudley?

ELIZABETH: Leicester. He is the Earl of Leicester.

BURLEIGH: Yes, Ma'am. Leicester. Why didn't you protect her?

ELIZABETH: It was nothing. A madman with a bucket of blood trying to get attention.

BURLEIGH: Are you alright, Gloriana?

ELIZABETH: I'm fine. I'm alright, aren't I, Shrewsbury?

SHREWSBURY: Yes, Ma'am.

DAVISON *is gaping at the Queen.*

ELIZABETH: Who are you? Little goldfish man …

DAVISON *continues to gape.*

What's wrong with him?

BURLEIGH: Answer Her Majesty, man.

DAVISON: I … My name is Davison, Your Highness …

Your Maje / sty—

BURLEIGH: Glori / ana.

DAVISON: Gloriana.

ELIZABETH: Oh, yes?

DAVISON: I am your new secretary, Ma'am.

ELIZABETH: Oh, yes. Hathborne died. Welcome.

DAVISON: Thank you, Your Majesty. Thank you.

ELIZABETH: Lovely.

DAVISON: Thank you.

BURLEIGH: That's enough, man.

DAVISON: Thank you.

He retreats to a corner.

BURLEIGH: Your Majesty, this could have been much worse. That bucket of blood could have been a knife. A pistol.

ELIZABETH: But it wasn't. It was a loon with a pail.

BURLEIGH: Your Grace, I don't wish to alarm you, but for every one of those stag madmen there is a *herd* of assassins biding their time, just waiting in the shadows.

ELIZABETH: Pardon?

BURLEIGH: We've received news of at least five other Catholic cells in the city. Enclaves of furious pope-worshipping rebels. They're no longer only in the north. They've reached London. Legions of them, in disguise.

ELIZABETH: What of it? I've never taken issue with them. My sister enjoyed staking Protestant heads to the bridge and burning clergy on a bonfire, but I have never taken part in such religious brutality. I have no desire to make windows into men's souls. It all ends up in God's hands in the end.

BURLEIGH: You say that, Majesty, but you have had the beacon of Catholicism locked away for nineteen years.

ELIZABETH: What beacon?

SHREWSBURY: Mary, Queen.

ELIZABETH: Beacon? Her?

BURLEIGH: Without question.

SHREWSBURY: She is much admired, Ma'am.

BURLEIGH: Much.

ELIZABETH: Leicester?

LEICESTER: She is a passing fashion, Bessie.

DAVISON: She is revered! Worshipped, even!

They all look at him. He falls back into silence.

BURLEIGH: You have imprisoned one of Rome's earthly angels, apparently.

ELIZABETH: She's not imprisoned because she's Catholic. She's imprisoned because she claimed my throne was hers and refuses to say otherwise.

LEICESTER: Over the years you have imprisoned her, Mary's star has risen slightly. But she doesn't blaze like you, Bess.

SHREWSBURY: She has become a saint to the Catholic / cause.

BURLEIGH: The longer we keep her out of sight, the more that star becomes a galaxy of rebel papists.

SHREWSBURY: To free her is their aim.

BURLEIGH: To put her on your throne is their purpose.

ELIZABETH: Enough of her people. What do my people want?

BURLEIGH: Her head, Your Majesty.

> *Beat.*

> *The other men look at him, shocked.*

They want the head of Stuart.

> *Beat.*

ELIZABETH: Her head?

BURLEIGH: Yes, Gloriana.

ELIZABETH: But … she's a queen.

BURLEIGH: She abdicated her throne. Her son sits on it now.

ELIZABETH: Little James.

BURLEIGH: Indeed.

ELIZABETH: He sent me a jewellery box.

BURLEIGH: He loves you very much.

ELIZABETH: He does, doesn't he?

BURLEIGH: You're like a mother to him.

ELIZABETH: I am, aren't I?

BURLEIGH: Indeed.

ELIZABETH: He asked me to marry him too. I said maybe.

LEICESTER: Oh, for God's sake.

ELIZABETH: He wants me as mother *and* as wife.

DAVISON: Should I be taking this down?

> *Beat.* ELIZABETH *stares at* BURLEIGH.

ELIZABETH: Her head, you say?

> *Silence.*

SHREWSBURY: Your Majesty. If I may / speak—

BURLEIGH: Shrewsbury, don't distract / Her Majesty.

ELIZABETH: Speak, Shrewsbury. Your counsel is most welcome.

SHREWSBURY: My Queen. This isle has never seen such prosperous days—you have brought peace and calm and beauty to this realm. Something past lords never could. Don't tarnish your pristine reign with the fallen head of an innocent sister queen.

BURLEIGH: Are you questioning the verdict of my / forty-two magistrates?

SHREWSBURY: Today's verdicts are not tomorrow's and are no longer yesterday's. A verdict tilts and turns and rises and falls in an ever-changing wave, Your Majesty. You have hated bloodshed in your reign, why bathe yourself in it now? You have the soft heart of a woman. God has given you sweetness and virtue. Use that now. This decision falls to no magistrates. This falls to you / alone.

BURLEIGH: Are you defending the criminal who has conspired against our queen's life? Does no-one here support Gloriana? The victim?

SHREWSBURY: Mary has had no lawyer. No-one has dared speak to her advantage. Mercy toward her has been silenced for nineteen years. You yourself have never seen her face, Your Highness. Nothing in your heart seems to speak for her.

BURLEIGH: How dare you question Gloriana's heart when Mary's beats inside a murderer's chest?

SHREWSBURY: I do not speak against Mary's guilt, Lord Burleigh. It is indeed suspected she had her husband murdered. It is true she wed his killer. But that happened at a dark, unfortunate time, in the shadow of civil war, where she, the weakest of creatures, as invaders advanced, had to seek protection in the most unlikely of places. Women are such frail beings and this world serves them too cruelly.

BURLEIGH: All the more reason to protect our queen.

ELIZABETH: A woman is not weak, gentlemen. There are plenty of strong souls amongst my sex. You look upon one now. I will hear no more of this 'weakness' you both speak of.

SHREWSBURY: Your Majesty, I—

BURLEIGH: Gloriana, you—

ELIZABETH: *Enough.* The both of you.

> Leicester.
>
> Tooth.

He kisses her.

Why are you so silent?

LEICESTER: I'm merely surprised, Bessie, that you allow your ears to be filled with such fairytales. No-one is coming to get you. There are no mobs. No plots. No-one is following an ageing countryless queen who hasn't been seen in decades. No-one would turn their back on you, a worshipped monarch, to follow a husband-killer and a mad-woman. You thrive daily as she withers away. You don't need her head. She's already dead.

Silence.

ELIZABETH: This head we speak of. What does it look like?

BURLEIGH: How do you mean, Ma'am?

ELIZABETH: Davison, have you seen her?

DAVISON: Only in pictures, Ma'am.

ELIZABETH: You can never trust pictures. What does she look like? Is she handsome?

The men glance around the room awkwardly.

I hear she has red hair. Like me. Burleigh.

BURLEIGH: Not quite as red as yours. More of an … auburn.

SHREWSBURY: Chestnut.

LEICESTER: Mahogany.

DAVISON: Like crackling flames.

Beat.

ELIZABETH: And her skin?

BURLEIGH: Sallow.

SHREWSBURY: Pale. Too pale.

DAVISON: Translucent. Luminous.

Beat.

ELIZABETH: And how tall?

SHREWSBURY: Surprisingly, actually, / Ma'am.

ELIZABETH: But *how* tall?

BURLEIGH: Oh, I'd say … about …

He holds his hand high. ELIZABETH *walks beneath it.*

ELIZABETH: She may be taller, but she has no advantage, for I have often been told I am exactly the right height.

LEICESTER: Indeed, Bessie.

ELIZABETH: How many attendants does she have?

BURLEIGH: Her women, Ma'am …

ELIZABETH: Women? She has female attendants?

BURLEIGH: Did. They were all removed from service.

ELIZABETH: Oh.

BURLEIGH: Even her jester.

ELIZABETH: She had a female jester?

BURLEIGH: Indeed.

ELIZABETH: Women aren't funny.

>   *Beat.*

What does she do all day? In there.

BURLEIGH: She used to read. But I had her books confiscated.

ELIZABETH: Why?

BURLEIGH: To prevent her mind being infiltrated by salacious literature, Majesty.

ELIZABETH: Ooh. Give them to me, I'd like to read them. What else does she do?

BURLEIGH: She sings. Plays with her dog.

ELIZABETH: I never got a dog when I was imprisoned.

BURLEIGH: She writes.

ELIZABETH: Writes what?

BURLEIGH: Poems.

ELIZABETH: Does she? I like poems.

SHREWSBURY: I know, Ma'am. You are a great supporter of the arts.

ELIZABETH: I am the greatest supporter of the arts. How many plays do we have here a week, Leicester.

LEICESTER: Many, Bessie. Many, many plays.

ELIZABETH: Perhaps I should commission a poem from her?

>   *She laughs. They join.*

And her weight?

>   *The men look at her awkwardly.*

Is she fat?

BURLEIGH: She is … the weight you would expect.

>   ELIZABETH *thinks.*

ELIZABETH: Huh.

PAULET *and* MORTIMER *arrive.*

Ah, Paulet. We were just talking about your fat prisoner Mary.

BURLEIGH: What are you doing here, Paulet?

PAULET: I am here to see Her Majesty.

BURLEIGH: What for?

PAULET: I have correspondence for / Her Majesty—

ELIZABETH: Who is this?

PAULET: My nephew.

MORTIMER: I am Mortimer, Your Majesty.

PAULET: He has just returned from battle.

ELIZABETH: Ah. Welcome home.

MORTIMER: It was an honour to serve in your name, Majesty.

ELIZABETH: England's name. Not mine.

BURLEIGH: Her Majesty doesn't care for talk of war.

ELIZABETH: I am perfectly capable of conversing on matters of warfare, Burleigh.

[*To* MORTIMER] Where did you serve, soldier?

MORTIMER: The Netherlands, Your Majesty.

ELIZABETH: Ah. Yes. Zutphen. Your silly little skirmish, Leicester.

MORTIMER *looks at* LEICESTER, *stunned.*

MORTIMER: Lieutenant-General?

LEICESTER: Soldier.

MORTIMER: I'm sorry, sir. I … didn't recognise you.

An awkward silence.

PAULET: Mortimer is assisting me with the prisoner, Your Highness.

ELIZABETH: Assisting you? What's wrong with you?

BURLEIGH: Gout, Majesty.

ELIZABETH: Oh. So you've met her? The conspirator.

MORTIMER: If you mean Mary Stuart, yes, Your Majesty, I have.

ELIZABETH: Tell me what you think of her.

MORTIMER: She … she is …

He falters.

I'm sorry, Your Majesty, it seems … distasteful to find words for someone as plain as Mary when I am standing in front of Gloriana herself.

ELIZABETH: Why have I never met your nephew before, Paulet?

PAULET: He has been travelling, Your Majesty. Since his service.

ELIZABETH: Oh, yes? Where?

MORTIMER: Asia. The Americas. Tartary. Bohemia. Which of those is your favourite destination, Majesty?

Another awkward silence.

SHREWSBURY: The Queen is not well-travelled.

ELIZABETH: You make me sound positively dull, Shrewsbury. I simply choose to remain within the bounds of my beloved realm so that my subjects always know I am near.
Tell me … did you go to Rome?

MORTIMER: I did. Undercover, of course. I pretended to be a Catholic.

ELIZABETH: How tiresome. What did you see there? Are they still practising their ridiculous rituals?

MORTIMER: If you mean are they still gathering in grotesquely hideous cathedrals to perform cheap wizardry with pieces of bread and cups of wine, yes they are, Your Majesty.

ELIZABETH: Ugh. And their makeshift God? How's he going?

MORTIMER: The Pope?

ELIZABETH: Yes. Him.

MORTIMER: As dull as ever. You should consider yourself lucky to be excommunicated, Your Majesty.

Silence.

ELIZABETH: I beg your pardon?

BURLEIGH: I was about to deliver that news, Ma'am. I was waiting for a moment alone with / you to—

ELIZABETH: Shut up, Burleigh. What did you say, Mortimer?

MORTIMER: The Pope. He … Your Majesty, the *Regnans in Excelsis* has been declared.

ELIZABETH: The what?

BURLEIGH: It's a papal bull, Your Majesty.

He gets out a piece of paper and reads.

'Elizabeth, the pretended Queen of England and the servant of crime, is declared a heretic. We charge and command that all nobles, subjects, peoples and others do not dare obey her orders, mandates and laws.'

ELIZABETH: 'Servant of crime'? What crime?

BURLEIGH: 'Only the Catholic Church shall provide salvation. The Pope alone is head of the earthly church. The ungodly have grown in power and Elizabeth has assisted in this. Furthermore, she has filled the Royal Council of England with obscure men.'

ELIZABETH: What obscure men?

Beat. Her obscure men say nothing.

BURLEIGH: 'We do, out of the fullness of our apostolic power, declare the aforesaid Elizabeth to be a heretic and favourer of heretics. She has thus incurred the sentence of excommunication and is hereby cut off from the unity of the body of Christ.'

ELIZABETH: You can't be excommunicated from a religion you never took part in. It's like a Jew telling me I've been banned from circumcision.

DAVISON: Should I write that / down—?

BURLEIGH, PAULET and LEICESTER: [*together*] No.

BURLEIGH *reads from the papal bull.*

BURLEIGH: 'Any attacks made on the False Queen will be viewed as God's will.'

Silence. BURLEIGH *hands the decree to* ELIZABETH.

ELIZABETH: So the Pope has put a price on my head?

[*To* LEICESTER] Robert, you said no-one was coming to get me.

[*To* SHREWSBURY] Today's verdicts are not tomorrow's and are no longer yesterday's, it seems, Shrewsbury.

Silence.

PAULET: Ma'am … if I may … I have another piece of correspondence for you.

ELIZABETH: And who is this one from? St Francis of Assisi? The arch-angel Gabriel?

PAULET: It's from Mary, Ma'am.

BURLEIGH: That should have gone through me.

PAULET: I'm her jailer.

BURLEIGH: The Queen is her jailer.

ELIZABETH: She is her own jailer. What is it?

PAULET: A letter, Your Majesty. She wrote it this afternoon.

ELIZABETH: She knows of the verdict?

PAULET and BURLEIGH: [*together*] She does, Your Majesty.

ELIZABETH: And of the possible sentence?

PAULET and BURLEIGH: [*together*] She does, Your Majesty.

ELIZABETH: And what was her response?

PAULET: She was … disheartened.

ELIZABETH: I see.

PAULET: She awaits your decision.

BURLEIGH: The punishment for treason is beheading.

SHREWSBURY: Not always. Not always.

ELIZABETH: Give me the letter.

> PAULET *does.*
>
> *Silence as* ELIZABETH *reads.*
>
> *She wipes away a tear.*
>
> *She looks at* SHREWSBURY *who is still standing partially covered in blood.*

That could have been my blood you're covered in, Shrewsbury.

SHREWSBURY: It's just pig blood, Ma'am. Or a cow.

ELIZABETH: Or a dog.

> *Silence.*

If I were to … punish her accordingly … it would send a strong sign, wouldn't it? All this noise echoing through the streets, keeping me awake at night. These madmen with buckets of blood … it would stop.

LEICESTER: Bessie, / there is no need for …

ELIZABETH: It would send a message to those cells. Those rebels. The Pope. I have been peaceful in the past, but I will defend my father's legacy.

SHREWSBURY: Your Majesty … be very careful. Please.

BURLEIGH: The Queen is more than capable of deciding for herself, Shrewsbury.

ELIZABETH: It seems the conspirator has already made up her mind as to her fate. And the magistrates have made up theirs. There's nothing more I can do about it. It's her crime and their verdict that will send her to the block.

PAULET: The law will still require your signature on the death warrant, Your Majesty. It is you who ultimately decides.

Beat.

ELIZABETH: Of course.

Of course.

I'd like to be alone now.

Go and wash yourself off, Shrewsbury.

Thank you.

BURLEIGH: Shall I take the letter, Your Majesty?

ELIZABETH: No. It's mine.

The men depart, except LEICESTER.

The young GIRL *remains. Ignored. Unseen.*

You. Mortimer. Stay.

MORTIMER *stays.*

Come here.

He does.

Then ...

The verdict is spoken and it must be done and I have to order the execution.

MORTIMER: It is a grave duty, Your Majesty.

ELIZABETH: Indeed.

Beat.

Did you experience much death? As a soldier?

MORTIMER: Many times.

ELIZABETH: What did you see? When you looked into the eyes of the man you had to kill?

MORTIMER: Only myself, Your Majesty. Reflected back at me, like a mirror. As if my enemy had captured my very soul and was taunting me with my own fearful image. And the only way to get my soul back was to smash that mirror.

Beat.

ELIZABETH: And when it comes, no matter if it's a bullet or a bomb, a death is a death, yes? In the end. No matter the method, we all take our last breath. We all live until the last moment of our life, however it is taken from us.

MORTIMER: Yes, Your Majesty. A death is a death.

ELIZABETH: If I can be murdered by a pope, she can be murdered by a man.

MORTIMER: Yes, Your Majesty.

ELIZABETH: If you can kill an enemy on the battleground, you can kill an enemy in a room.

MORTIMER: Yes, Your Majesty.

ELIZABETH: Because a death is a death.

MORTIMER: Yes, Your Majesty.

ELIZABETH: I do not wish to sign her death warrant.

MORTIMER: Yes.

ELIZABETH: Yet, with my entire being, I want that mirror smashed. Because what we appear to be is subject to great judgement. And what we really are is not.

MORTIMER: Yes, Gloriana.

ELIZABETH: And yet a death is a death.

Silence.

Thank you, sir. Good day.

He goes to leave.

Mortimer. Remember that the tender works of secrecy form the closest bonds.

She offers her cheek. MORTIMER *kisses it. Leaves.*

LEICESTER: Bessie.

ELIZABETH: What?

LEICESTER: You don't need him. You don't know him.

ELIZABETH: I feel I do. I need protection. He's a soldier.

LEICESTER: So am I.

ELIZABETH: There's something about him. His eyes …

LEICESTER: Bessie. Hear me. Please.

He pulls her to him gently.

I would never let any man harm you.

ELIZABETH: I fear no *man*, Robert …

ELIZABETH *looks at Mary's letter.*

LEICESTER: She's got no country. No crown. No-one.

ELIZABETH: She haunts me.
   If I dare sleep I dream of her.
   When I wake, I hear her name echoing through the streets.
   She invades me.

SCENE TWO: MARY / ELIZABETH

MARY *prays softly.*

Her dog is nearby.

MARY: *Pater noster, qui es in caelis, sanctificetur nomen tuum. Adveniat regnum tuum. Fiat voluntas tua, sicut in caelo et in terra. Panem nostrum quotidianum da nobis hodie, et dimitte nobis debita nostra sicut et nos dimittimus debitoribus nostris. Et ne nos inducas in tentationem, sed libera nos a malo. Amen. Pater noster, qui es in caelis, sanctificetur nomen tuum ...*

   Calls and noise from outside.

   MARY *goes to the window.*

   Stands in front of it.

   A crowd cheers.

   Meanwhile ...

   The young GIRL *stands nearby. Watching.*

   ELIZABETH *hears the voices.*

   She peers out of the window at the gathering crowds.

   The chant echoes and morphs ...

   Meanwhile ...

   MARY *adopts a picture of mournfulness at her window.*

   Head angled just so. Hands clasped in prayer.

   Her lips continue moving in conversation with God.

   As she prays and poses, the voices surge with excitement ...

   ELIZABETH *stands at her own window and watches, coldly.*

   The two women pray accompanied by a cacophony of cries outside. As they do, the young GIRL *brings them meals covered by a linen cloth.*

Adveniat regnum tuum. Fiat voluntas tua, sicut in caelo et in terra. Panem nostrum quotidianum da nobis hodie, et dimitte nobis debita nostra sicut et nos dimittimus debitoribus nostris. Et ne nos inducas in tentationem, Sed libera nos a malo.

ELIZABETH: [*concurrently*] Our Father who art in Heaven, hallowed be Thy name. Thy Kingdom come, Thy will be done on earth as it is in Heaven. Give us this day our daily bread and forgive us our trespasses as we forgive those who trespass against us, and lead us not into temptation but deliver us from evil.

Both women move to their meals.

ELIZABETH *and* MARY *lift the linen cloths to reveal bread and wine.*

They drink the wine.

They eat the bread.

Separated by space ...

Yet so close they could touch ...

END OF ACT TWO

ACT THREE

SCENE ONE

A party.

Revellers fill the stage in elaborate costumes and masks.

The greatest party there has ever been.

Music.

Dancing.

Drugs.

Booze.

Sex.

The revellers move amongst one another until finally, from amidst them,
ELIZABETH *emerges with* LEICESTER.

They are outside ...

ELIZABETH: Oh, Leicester! What a party!

LEICESTER: Anything for you, Bessie.

ELIZABETH: I think I'm quite drunk.

LEICESTER: Good. You deserve a little fun.

ELIZABETH: I do, don't I?

LEICESTER: How's your tooth?

ELIZABETH: Sore. Kiss it better.

    He does.

  Do I taste good?

LEICESTER: Always.

ELIZABETH: I think I'm quite drunk. Did I say that already?

    LEICESTER *fills up her glass.*

LEICESTER: You just need a little sun and air.

    ELIZABETH *cracks up.*

ELIZABETH: I do need a little son and heir! You funny bastard.

    She kisses him again.

LEICESTER: Now sit down. I'm going to tell you a story. Then I'm going to give you a gift.

ELIZABETH: Are you?! How marvellous! Another drink?

He tops her up.

LEICESTER: Why not? Ready? Good.
      Echo was a nymph who served Hera.

ELIZABETH: Oh, God. Is this one of those dull Greek fairytales?

LEICESTER: Shhh, Bessie. Hera was queen of all the gods.

ELIZABETH: I'm a queen.

LEICESTER: Indeed you are, my darling Bess.
      Echo was expected to give Hera her unwavering and eternal loyalty and devotion. But Echo had a bad habit. She loved a chat. Echo liked to talk about all sorts of things … Politics. Poetry. Love. Ambition. Echo loved to talk and talk and talk.

ELIZABETH: Ugh.

LEICESTER: Queen Hera did not. There was something about the nymph that incensed her. The incessant chatter. That voice … always in her ear … And Hera noticed that people seemed to listen to Echo more than her—their own queen.

ELIZABETH: Poor queen.

LEICESTER: And so she cursed Echo. She saw to it that the nymph was silenced. She made sure that Echo could no longer voice her own words and thoughts. Only repeat what others had said.

ELIZABETH *laughs.*

For some reason, this made Echo even more desirable. She was still a pretty little nymph, after all. Somehow men desired her even more without her voice. But they used her curse against her.
      'I want you', they'd say. And Echo would have to repeat it back to them, even though they knew it wasn't what she desired.

He straddles ELIZABETH.

'I want you … you're mine' they'd say, and Echo would say it right back. Go on.

ELIZABETH: 'I want you … you're mine …'

LEICESTER: 'Take me. I'm yours', they'd say. And she'd say …

ELIZABETH: 'Take me. I'm yours.'

LEICESTER: 'Fuck me', they'd say. 'Fuck me.' And she'd have to reply …

ELIZABETH: 'Fuck me.' 'Fuck me ...'

LEICESTER: Those men tore her body into little pieces, that nymph, until all that remained was her voice echoing through the forest.

He smiles down at her.

ELIZABETH: Why did you tell me that story?

A masked guest speaks as ECHO.

ECHO: Why did you tell me that story?

ELIZABETH *looks shocked.*

ELIZABETH: What was that?

ECHO: What was that?

ELIZABETH *gasps.*

So does ECHO.

LEICESTER: I got you your very own Echo, my Queen.

ELIZABETH: An echo? For me?

ECHO: An echo? For me?

LEICESTER *looks at the masked guests.*

LEICESTER: Which one do you think it is? Which one of these guests is *your* Echo, Queen Hera?

ELIZABETH: I don't know.

ECHO: I don't know.

ELIZABETH *laughs. She walks up to a guest.*

ELIZABETH: Is it this one?

ECHO: Is it this one?

LEICESTER: Not that one.

ELIZABETH: Is it this one?

ECHO: Is it this one?

LEICESTER: No.

ELIZABETH: This one!

ECHO: This one!

ELIZABETH: Oh, Robert, what a / wild gift!

ECHO: Oh, Robert, what a wild gift!

He starts kissing her neck.

ELIZABETH: I think I'm / quite drunk.

ECHO: I think I'm quite drunk.

ELIZABETH: My echo is making / me woozy.

ECHO: My echo is making me woozy.

ELIZABETH: Which fucking / one is it?

ECHO: Which fucking one is it?

ELIZABETH: I think I might need / some food.

ECHO: I think I might need some food.

> LEICESTER *is on top of* ELIZABETH.

ELIZABETH: Robert, / stop.

ECHO: Robert, stop.

ELIZABETH: I'm feeling / quite ...

ECHO: I'm feeling quite ...

ELIZABETH: Ro / bert ...

ECHO: Robert ...

ELIZABETH: Robert, / get off me ...

ECHO: Robert, get off me ...

ELIZABETH: *Robert / Dudley!*

ECHO: *Robert Dudley!*

> LEICESTER *gets off her, furious.*

LEICESTER: Elizabeth, I want to *fuck* you!

ELIZABETH: Robert, keep your / voice down.

ECHO: Robert, keep your voice down.

LEICESTER: It's been decades, Bess. Surely the foreplay is over.

ELIZABETH: Rob / ert!

ECHO: Robert!

LEICESTER: Elizabeth, I have loved you since the day we met.

ELIZABETH: And I / love you.

ECHO: And I love you.

ELIZABETH: Which fucking one is it?

ECHO: Which fucking one is it?

LEICESTER: I have waited and waited and waited. I have watched you court the Crowns of Europe, I have heard you swear your love for strangers, I have been your constant companion for three decades. I am the closest thing you have to a husband. So make me your husband. I am the closest thing you have to a lover. So make me your lover. Bess, please.

He pushes her to the ground, kisses her.

ELIZABETH: You're just frustrated, / Robert.

ECHO: You're just frustrated, Robert.

ELIZABETH: You're still embarrassed about what happened / in the Netherlands.

ECHO: You're still embarrassed about what happened in the Netherlands.

LEICESTER: No more of that, Elizabeth, / please ...

His advances become more insistent.

ELIZABETH: I should have just gone there myself. / Taken care of things.

ECHO: I should have just gone there myself. Taken care of things.

LEICESTER: You think you could've done it better, Bess?

He's getting rougher.

ELIZABETH: Of course not, my darling / lieutenant general.

ECHO: Of course not, my darling lieutenant / general.

LEICESTER: Just keep still, Bessie.

She struggles against him.

ELIZABETH: Careful, Robert ...

ECHO: Careful, Robert ...

ELIZABETH: Robert, stop now. / Please.

ECHO: Robert, stop now. / Please.

ELIZABETH: I'm the Virgin Queen.

ECHO: I'm the Virgin Queen.

ELIZABETH: I'm the Virgin / Queen!

ECHO: I'm the Virgin Queen!

He gets off her, furious.

LEICESTER: You are not a virgin, Elizabeth! You are a frigid fifty-four-year-old equivocator!

ELIZABETH: How dare / you.

ECHO: How dare / you.

ELIZABETH: I'm the / Queen!

ECHO: I'm the / Queen!

ELIZABETH: I'm Glori / ana!

ECHO: I'm Glori / ana!

ELIZABETH: I'm the *Queen*!

ECHO: I'm the *Queen*!

> *He is gone.*
>
> *The* QUEEN *is alone at her own party.*
>
> *Except for ...*
>
> *One guest, who appears seemingly from nowhere.*

ELIZABETH: Are you my echo?

ECHO: Are you my echo?

ELIZABETH: Who are you?

ECHO: Who are you?

ELIZABETH: I'm the Queen.

ECHO: I'm the Queen.

ELIZABETH: I'm the Queen.

ECHO: I'm the Queen.

ELIZABETH: Take off your mask.

ECHO: Take off your mask.

ELIZABETH: I mean it. Take off your mask.

ECHO: I mean it. Take off your mask.

ELIZABETH: I am Queen Hera, Echo. Take off that fucking mask.

> *Silence.*
>
> *The* ECHO *removes her mask.*
>
> *It's* MARY.

MARY: Hello.

ELIZABETH: Hello.

> It's you.

MARY: It's you.

ELIZABETH: What are you doing at my party?

MARY: God answered my prayers.

ELIZABETH: Robert! Robert!

> ELIZABETH *goes to run.* MARY *stops her.*

MARY: Please. Don't.

> I just want to talk to you. My sister-cousin. Queen to queen.
> Please, dearest Bessie.
>
> Let's get a little sun and air together at last.

> *The two women stare at one another.*

A long moment.

ELIZABETH: You're not fat at all.

Silence.

Well. Speak.

Beat.

MARY: How are you?

ELIZABETH: I have a sore tooth.

MARY: I'm sorry to hear that.

ELIZABETH: Thank you.

Beat.

How are you?

MARY: Tired.

ELIZABETH: Me too. I think I've had too much to drink.

MARY: It's a good party.

ELIZABETH: Would you like some wine?

MARY: I'd love some. Thank you.

ELIZABETH *pours.*

ELIZABETH: The blood of Christ.

MARY: Ha.

ELIZABETH: I used to love that bit. Of Mass.

MARY: Really?

ELIZABETH: I used to go with my sister. Not because I wanted to. I just didn't want to make her angry. She had a foul temper. All you Catholics do. But I did quite enjoy the bread and wine stuff. It was like a wonderful magic trick in the middle of a really boring show.

MARY: The consecration is indeed miraculous.

ELIZABETH: I was always jealous of the priest, though. Why did God choose *him* to speak through? Why him when I was there? And not just that man. Countless men. All over the world. In their frocks, performing 'miracles' in the name of a God who was supposed to belong to all of us. I could never understand it. Still tasted like sour wine and stale bread to me. Nothing miraculous in that.

MARY: However His body and blood may taste to you, God deserves glory. He deserves earthly royalty to kneel before Him as a reminder that although they are kings and queens and princes and princesses they are still mortal. They are still His children, just as the plain man in the robe is His child, just as the beggar in the street is His child, just as the sick, the poor, the imprisoned are His children. He has given us life. The least we can do is bow our heads in humility, just for a moment, and honour all He has forsaken, all He has sacrificed, all He is.

Silence.

ELIZABETH: I do.

MARY: What?

ELIZABETH: Honour God. If anything, we honour Him more. We honour His book, not rituals created by men to suit their own vanities. We honour the one Lord—not a man sitting on an Italian throne surrounded by conspiracy and cover-ups and obscene displays of wealth. We pray to God—not to long-dead levitating and hallucinating lunatics. Not to criminals and madmen and red-robed charlatans. And we certainly don't demean God's infinite power with prayers to a surrogate saint named Mary.

Beat.

MARY: Of course. Why would anyone put their faith in a self-proclaimed Virgin Mother?

Silence.

ELIZABETH: I will fight to maintain my faith. It deserves to thrive. And we will not be quashed by a Catholic Goliath.

MARY: Don't make yourselves the underdogs, Elizabeth. We are the ones being driven into hiding.

ELIZABETH: I have *always* been the underdog, Mary.

MARY: Since when?

ELIZABETH: Since I was born a woman. Since the first look of disappointment on my father's fat face. Since my mother's execution for being a whore and a witch. Since being sent away to live as an orphan and a pauper, in the houses of strange men with strange ways. Since I was imprisoned by my own sister for being a threat to her throne. Living every day wondering if it was my last. Since taking the crown and having to fight to keep it on my head. Against men. Against women. Against you, sitting there in a French court wearing *two* crowns on your head, surrounded by wealth and education and comfort and adoration and love.

Since then, Mary.

I may be Queen. And you may be imprisoned. But I have suffered infinitely more than you.

Silence.

MARY: Elizabeth.

Nineteen years ago I came to you for help. I was your equal. I was queen of a country. You were queen of a country. The same blood courses through our veins. We wrote intimate letters to one another. I came to you in fear and in need. I asked for your hospitality and was assured I would receive it.

Instead, you tore my request to shreds.

You locked me away from the whole world. You took away my freedom. You denied me access to my people, to my friends, to my allies.

You placed your thumb over my head and ground me and my God-given rights into the dirt.

ELIZABETH: I have to protect my people and their faith.

MARY: You don't care about your people. You don't care about God.

ELIZABETH: I am queen of the people. I reign in God's name.

MARY: The only name you reign in is your own. And you're not even satisfied with having just one. Queen Elizabeth. Good Queen Bess. The Virgin Queen. Gloriana.

ELIZABETH: Those names are what my people call me. I have no control over that.

MARY: You have full control, Elizabeth. Which is exactly what you've always wanted.

I have one title. Mary Stuart.

And I have no control over that name or its legacy. Because you've locked it away. Silenced it.

Beat.

I like sitting here with you, Elizabeth. Outside.

ELIZABETH: As do I, Mary.

MARY *shifts uncomfortably.*

Are you alright?

MARY: Yes. Pains.

ELIZABETH: Oh. I have the stomach of a king.

They sit together quietly. They drink.

Why do you wish me dead?

MARY: I do not wish death upon anyone.

ELIZABETH: You have been found guilty of conspiring to have me murdered.

MARY: I would never murder a queen.

ELIZABETH: Why not? You had your own husband murdered.

MARY: Eliza / beth—

ELIZABETH: Then married his killer.

MARY: Eliza / beth—

ELIZABETH: Hope he washed the blood off his hands before he fucked you. Leaves a nasty stain, blood. We're proof of that.

MARY: I didn't have Darnley murdered. He simply made too many enemies in his life. And I didn't choose to marry Bothwell after he killed Darnley. I didn't choose to be kidnapped by him, tied down and raped by him. I didn't choose to be dragged down the aisle still in my mourning dress. I did choose to ask for a knife on my wedding night to cut my throat with, but I reckoned suicide would just put me in Hell with more of both their kind. I didn't choose to have my Scottish subjects turn on me. I didn't choose to be ignored by my French allies. I didn't choose to be called 'whore' by the whole world. I didn't choose for those twins that were raped into me to bleed out of me. But I did choose to run. If you think running is a choice. I ran. To you. For assistance. Only to have any choice at all taken from me for the next nineteen years.

ELIZABETH: Are you finished?

Beat.

Because you seem to have skipped some other 'choices'.

Such as choosing to sign a treaty that claimed you were the Queen of England.

MARY: I was a child. I didn't know what I was signing.

ELIZABETH: And choosing to *not* sign a treaty that declared I was Queen of England.

MARY: I simply didn't agree with every clause.

ELIZABETH: And choosing to engage in correspondence with known terrorists.

MARY: The signature on those letters is forged. I would never commit regicide against a fellow queen.

ELIZABETH: And choosing to infect the minds and hearts of my subjects.

MARY: How could I possibly do that when I have spent every hour of the last two decades caged like an animal?

ELIZABETH: You know. By appearing at your window. Letting the outside world catch a glimpse of you. A picture of mournfulness. Your head angled just so. Your hands clasped in prayer. Your lips moving as you speak to God, asking Him to forgive their queen for the torment she is inflicting upon you. All the while planning my death. Fantasising about my crown on your head. Your cunt on my throne.

Silence. They drink.

MARY: How old were you when your mother died, Elizabeth?

ELIZABETH: Nearly three.

MARY: Can't have been easy. Knowing that your father ordered her execution. Then all those stepmothers that came and went.

ELIZABETH: I wasn't close to many of them.

MARY: Was he a good father? Henry.

ELIZABETH: He was, eventually. When my mother was beheaded he made sure to order the finest executioner in the world. Had him shipped over from France. And he proved his worth. One blow and she was gone.

MARY: I never met my father. I was only six days old when he died. His final words were, 'Alas. I have a lass.'

They both laugh. They drink.

How is my son?

ELIZABETH: He's very well.

MARY: Please send him my regards.

ELIZABETH: I will.

MARY: What's he like?

ELIZABETH: Podgy. Chaste. Protestant.

MARY: Does he have a lover?

ELIZABETH: Strangely, no.

MARY: Is he happy?

ELIZABETH: Seems to be.

MARY: The last time I held him, he wasn't even a year old.

ELIZABETH: He's nearly twenty now.

MARY: I can still remember holding his head in my hands. The smell of his skin.

ELIZABETH: You needn't worry. We have a very close relationship. He signs every letter, 'Your compatriot and son, James'. Very sweet.

Beat.

He looks like you. Not Darnley. Just so you know.

MARY: Thank you. Shall we go in?

ELIZABETH: No. I like it.

MARY: Me too.

Beat. They sit together.

Why did you stop writing to me, Bessie?

ELIZABETH: I've been a little bit busy, Mary.

MARY: Why did you never come and visit me? Or have me come to you?

ELIZABETH: Because you're not entitled to visits. What did you expect? Afternoon tea with the Queen of England? Claret and cake and a quick game of skittles? You're a terrorist, woman! A criminal! Good Lord! You think you've got it so hard, don't you? You've got a dog! I never had a dog when I was imprisoned!

She drinks.

I was sailed past the decapitated heads on the bridge that my sister had staked there. Then up through Traitors Gate. Past a line of armed men. Leering at me. Spitting in my face. Calling me names. Past the scaffold of Jane Grey, that poor girl forced by ambitious men to claim my sister's throne as her own. I walked through her blood, that little girl. I took her place in the Tower. Saw so many names scratched into the walls by women whose only crime was womanhood. Jane Grey. Margaret of Anjou. Anne Askew. Margaret Pole. My aunt Jane Rochford. My stepmother Catherine Howard.

And my mother. Anne Boleyn.

I sat with the ghosts of those women for two whole months. I talked to them. Prayed to them. Cried for them. As I waited for my sister the Queen to decide my fate.

MARY: Two months.

ELIZABETH: Two months. My sister left me in the Tower for two months.

> *Beat.*

But I survived.

My name isn't scratched into any prison walls, like those women before me.

I'm Queen.

MARY: Does this mean you will show me the mercy your sister showed you?

> *Silence.*

Please give me my life back, Elizabeth. You have won. You are Queen. I renounce any claim to your throne, real or fabricated. You can have all the supremacy you desire. But please give me my life back.

Please let me go home.

To Scotland.

To my son.

Say, 'You are free, Mary'.

'You are free, Mary.'

Elizabeth, please say, 'You are free, Mary'.

ELIZABETH: You are …

> *She stares at* MARY.

… not at all like I expected.

I mean, where is the beauty I heard so much about?

The face that the Pope himself would murder a queen for.

You're quite plain.

You've aged.

You look weak.

Weary.

Defeated by life.

MARY: Elizabeth. I hold no vanity in my soul. Your taunts don't touch me. I have no fear of ageing. I only fear that I won't age.

> *Beat.*

ELIZABETH: Then you should be thanking me.

MARY: Why?

ELIZABETH: Because you'd be dead without me.

You were homeless, Mary. I took you in. Saved you from your own stupid choices, your own squandered privileges. You have been safer these past nineteen years than you've ever been in your life. If I hadn't given you refuge you would have been torn apart, limb from limb. Your entrails scattered across the Channel. That is how reviled you were.

So don't ask me to save you. I already did. When God turned His back on you through shame, I opened my arms, offered my bosom and took you in. I'm not about to return you to a life of danger, Mary.

So I will keep keeping you.

Like a naughty little puppy.

If anything, to save you from yourself.

Silence.

MARY: Thank you, Gloriana.

Thank you, Virgin Queen.

Beat. MARY *flares.*

But I will not be shamed by the daughter of a man who changed God's word just so he could stick his cock inside your mother.

I will not be shamed by someone who came from the whoring loins of Anne Boleyn.

I will not be shamed by someone masquerading as a virgin when we all know you carried a child at fourteen.

ELIZABETH: How dare you.

MARY: Did he make you feel loved, your stepfather, after your mother had lost her head, and Henry refused to see you for all those years? / Did he say kind things as he tiptoed into your room every night and climbed into your bed? Did he hold you in a fatherly embrace as he fucked you?

She climbs on top of ELIZABETH.

ELIZABETH: Please stop. Stop it. Stop it. Stop it. Stop …

MARY: You must have made him want it. You must have given some kind of signal to him. You were at your ripest then, weren't you? / Tall, beautiful, pale-skinned, red-haired Princess Elizabeth.

ELIZABETH: Help me! Someone, please help! Help!

MARY *straddles* ELIZABETH.

MARY: Where did it end up, that baby? Will we see it on the throne one day like its bastard mother? Like Good Queen Fucking Bess Glori-fucking-ana!

ELIZABETH: Take your hands off / me!

ELIZABETH struggles to wrench herself free but MARY *is too strong.*

MARY: Your own father's laws make you an imposter.

The blood in my veins runs straight to the throne.

I was Queen of France. I was Queen of Scotland. And I am Queen of England.

So say it. Call me Queen.

ELIZABETH: No.

MARY: Call me Queen.

ELIZABETH: *No!*

MARY: Say, 'You are Queen'.

She forces her hand up ELIZABETH's *skirt.* ELIZABETH *gasps.*

ELIZABETH: You are Queen …

MARY: You are Queen!

ELIZABETH: You are Queen.

MARY: *You are Queen!*

ELIZABETH: *You are Queen! You are Queen! You are Queen! You are Queen! You are Queen! You are Queen! You are Queen! You are—*

MARY *is gone.*

Instead, a MAN *stands before her. He wears an executioner's mask. His torso is bare. He is covered in tattoos—images of Catholicism. Just like* MORTIMER.

He raises a pistol.

ELIZABETH *struggles to her feet.*

Starts to run.

Blackout.

Gunshot.

END OF ACT THREE

ACT FOUR

SCENE ONE: ELIZABETH

LEICESTER, MORTIMER, SHREWSBURY, AUBESPINE *and* DAVISON *are in panic mode.*

The young GIRL *is there too.*

LEICESTER: Is she dead? / Is she dead?

DAVISON: What do I tell people? I'm not sure what I—

AUBESPINE: I need to inform / the Dauphin—

SHREWSBURY: [*weeping*] My Queen … / My Queen …

LEICESTER: I only left her for a moment. I promise you, / I thought she'd be safe there …

MORTIMER: Who was responsible? Have they been caught? / Where are they being held?

AUBESPINE: Who is Queen now? Who is Queen now?! If Gloriana is dead, who is Queen now?

BURLEIGH enters.

They await his answer.

BURLEIGH: The Queen … is alive.

The men exhale.

She was wounded. The bullet grazed her neck.
She is being attended to.
The Queen is alive.

MORTIMER: Who is responsible?

BURLEIGH: We're still searching, but it's suspected he is a member of a French cell.

AUBESPINE: What? No, no, no, no, no, no, no / —

DAVISON: Shall I take this down?

BURLEIGH: A supporter of Mary Stuart's. He'd come in disguise.

SHREWSBURY: To the party?

AUBESPINE: No … no, no, no, no, / no, no—

LEICESTER: It was a fancy-dress party, old man. Everyone was in disguise.

BURLEIGH: The question is, why was she left alone in the first place?

DAVISON: I'll just take it down anyway.

BURLEIGH: Why was the Queen of England outside in a garden, drunk and under the influence of compounds, in the presence of a disguised French assassin?

SHREWSBURY: Compounds? / The Queen was stupefied?

AUBESPINE: Oh, no, no, no, / no, no—

LEICESTER: She wasn't stupefied. She was a little intoxicated, perhaps, / but …

SHREWSBURY: Stupefying compounds?

DAVISON: I probably shouldn't take that down, should I?

LEICESTER: I didn't see her imbibe anything but wine. I only wanted her to have a good time. She's been under a great deal of pressure. Where is she? I need to see her.

BURLEIGH: You're not going anywhere near her. You've proved yourself as useless here as you were in Europe, Dudley.

LEICESTER: How dare you, Burleigh. And my name / is—

BURLEIGH: My apologies—'Earl of Leicester'. 'Master of the Horse'. 'Lord Steward of Her Majesty'. 'Governor-General of the United Provinces'. Are there any other ridiculous titles I've missed there, / Robert?

LEICESTER: Is she alright? Just tell me if she's / alright!

BURLEIGH: No, she's not alright! She's completely delusional. When we found her, howling and bleeding in the garden, she was convinced she'd been talking to Mary Stuart.

SHREWSBURY: Good Lord.

AUBESPINE: *Mary Stuart?!*

BURLEIGH: She was hysterical. Screaming. 'Mary! Mary!'

MORTIMER: It wasn't Mary. She slept the night through. I kept watch.

BURLEIGH: *You* kept watch?

MORTIMER: My uncle needed a night with his family.

BURLEIGH: His job is to watch Mary Stuart.

MORTIMER: Mary slept soundly the whole night through. I watched her with my own eyes.

BURLEIGH: The Queen had to be sedated. Hysterical.

SHREWSBURY: Where is she now?

BURLEIGH: Sleeping.

LEICESTER: She never sleeps.

BURLEIGH: Resting.

LEICESTER: She never rests.

BURLEIGH: She should never have been left alone. Why on earth would you leave her / alone, Robert?

LEICESTER: I am *Leicester*!

MORTIMER: This man abandoned the Queen in a garden. How do we know he didn't orchestrate this assassination attempt?

LEICESTER: Because she's *mine*! She's *mine*! She's *mine*!

A shocked silence.

BURLEIGH: She's *yours*?

LEICESTER: I take care of her. She's my Bess.

MORTIMER: Is that why you got her drunk? Gave her delusional compounds? Organised a ridiculous party where anyone could walk in, aim a pistol at her head and fire? You should be strung up for what's happened, man. This is all your fault.

BURLEIGH: Now, gentlemen, enough.

MORTIMER: You may as well have pulled the trigger yourself.

LEICESTER: I take care of her!

MORTIMER: You are nothing but an incubus. Milking her. Like a useless fucking / child.

SHREWSBURY: Your Majesty!

ELIZABETH *is there.*

Her hair and dress are damp.

She is covered in blood.

Dazed.

LEICESTER: Bessie.

He moves toward her. She puts up her hand to stop him.

SHREWSBURY: Your Majesty, are you alright?

ELIZABETH: Yes, thank you.

SHREWSBURY: Your Highness … I think we should get you out of those bloody clothes.

ELIZABETH: No.

SHREWSBURY: You'll catch your death, Ma'am.

ELIZABETH: Is there a crowd outside, Shrewsbury?

SHREWSBURY: Yes, Ma'am.

ELIZABETH: Good. Let them see me.

> ELIZABETH *stands in front of the window.*
>
> *A picture of mournfulness. Head angled just so. Hands clasped in prayer.*
>
> *Her lips moving in silent conversation with God. 'Our Father ...'*
>
> *Voices from outside surge.*
>
> *She smiles at her subjects.*
>
> *Waves.*
>
> *Moves away from the window.*
>
> *Turns to* AUBESPINE.

What are you still doing here?

AUBESPINE: Your Majesty?

ELIZABETH: I don't want any hideous frogs in my court.

AUBESPINE: Madam ...

ELIZABETH: You're probably all in on it. You and that bitch prisoner and the Dauphin and the King. You don't want my hand in marriage. You only want my crown. Fuck off.

AUBESPINE: But, Your Majesty—

ELIZABETH: I said fuck off, you disgusting little man. You foul fucking Frenchman. And tell the Dauphin and his prick-sucking brother the King that *this* Queen lives. *This* Queen is alive. This Queen reigns on and will outlive the both of them. *Go!* Fucking *au revoir*!

> AUBESPINE *leaves.*

[*To* DAVISON] What's your name again?

DAVISON: Davison, Majesty.

ELIZABETH: Davison. I need a mirror.

> ELIZABETH *walks to him. She holds his chin in her hands and looks into his eyes.*
>
> *Moves onto* SHREWSBURY. *Does the same.*
>
> *To* BURLEIGH.
>
> *To* LEICESTER.
>
> *And finally ...*

To MORTIMER.

ELIZABETH *strokes his face.*

LEICESTER *watches on, seething.*

LEICESTER: Bessie.
ELIZABETH: You're very handsome, Mortimer.
MORTIMER: Thank you, Ma'am.
ELIZABETH: Your eyes. They're quite beguiling. I can see myself in them.
SHREWSBURY: Your Majesty, are you feeling alright?
ELIZABETH: At least, I think it's me …
Or is my enemy taunting me with my own fearful image?
MORTIMER: My eyes only reflect your supreme majesty, Gloriana.

She begins to loosen his shirt.

Ma'am …

She keeps undressing him.

Please, Ma'am. Gloriana.

MORTIMER *suddenly grabs her wrists.*

ELIZABETH *steps back.*

ELIZABETH: Hold him.

The other men hesitate.

MORTIMER: Don't touch me.
ELIZABETH: Hold him!

The other men obey.

MORTIMER *struggles.*

ELIZABETH *removes his shirt.*

He is covered in tattoos. Catholic icons.

This is the man.

She walks away.

Suddenly, MORTIMER *lunges at* ELIZABETH.

LEICESTER *stops him.*

Strangles him. It is a long and protracted death.

They all watch.

Silence.

DAVISON*'s pen is poised in horror.*

DAVISON: Do I … shall I … take that …?

Silence.

PAULET *arrives. Looks at the scene before him, stunned.*

PAULET: What is this?

LEICESTER: Your damn nephew tried to kill the Queen!

PAULET: What? No! What is this? What is this?

LEICESTER: He's not a soldier. He's a fucking deceiver. Look at him!

PAULET: I had no idea. Your Majesty, / I had no idea.

BURLEIGH: What are your intentions, Paulet?

PAULET: What do you mean?

BURLEIGH: How do we know you're not as depraved as your nephew?

PAULET: Because I … / because I … I …

BURLEIGH: You've been in her company for nineteen years. Has she be-
    guiled you, man? Have you perhaps fallen in love with your own /
    prisoner?

PAULET: No. No!

BURLEIGH: The witch has got to him too, / Gloriana. You'll be executed
    / for this, Paulet.

PAULET: No! Please.

    Your Majesty—if I were a traitor—if I loved my prisoner—I
    would not deliver this!

    He holds out piece of paper.

It is Mary Stuart's death warrant.

BURLEIGH: Give it to me. I should be delivering that. I'm head of the
    Privy Council.

PAULET: I'm her jailer.

BURLEIGH: Hand it over, man.

PAULET: I will only hand it to the Queen.

BURLEIGH: Give it to / me—

PAULET: It's not your / job to—

ELIZABETH: Let me see it.

    PAULET *hands* ELIZABETH *the paper.*

    She reads it.

BURLEIGH: All we need is your signature, Ma'am.

SHREWSBURY: The Queen needs time to think.

BURLEIGH: We don't have time. The citizens are restless.

SHREWSBURY: They've waited nineteen years, they can wait a little longer.

PAULET: My prisoner—Mary—would like to know sooner rather than later what her fate might be. She is ... quite fragile.

BURLEIGH: Fragile?! Your people are surrounding the palace, Ma'am. They nearly lost their queen today. They want to avenge you.

SHREWSBURY: Be careful, Elizabeth. I have watched your father and your sister sign lives away. It brings nothing but despair to everyone. You know that.

BURLEIGH: Shut up, / old man.

SHREWSBURY: Mary dead is far more powerful than Mary alive. Elizabeth, please be / careful.

BURLEIGH: Please, Majesty. Sign. The papists have awoken. They are at your door, thirsting for your / blood.

SHREWSBURY: Elizabeth. Do not sign. It will bring you no / peace.

LEICESTER: She's already dead, Bessie. She's been dead for nineteen / years.

SHREWSBURY: Your / Majesty.

PAULET: Good Queen / Bess.

LEICESTER: Our / Virgin.

BURLEIGH: Gloriana.

ELIZABETH: Leave me.

They do not move.

I said leave me.

The men start to depart. LEICESTER *stays.*

You too, Leicester.

LEICESTER: But, Bessie.

ELIZABETH: Go. Take him with you.

All the men depart, carrying MORTIMER'*s corpse from the room.*

The young GIRL *stays behind. Watching.*

ELIZABETH *speaks. Perhaps to herself. Perhaps to the* GIRL. *Perhaps to God. Perhaps to us ... As she does, she removes her wig and washes herself of blood.*

I am a slave.
  To my mind.
  To my sex.
  To my blood.
  To the service of my people.
  To my mother's legend.
  To my father's legacy ...
  The man who changed God's will to conceive me, only to deny my very right to exist.
  I have battled men my entire life. Kings. Suitors. Stepfathers. Assassins. Popes. I have allied myself with an invisible army of Elizabeths as my protection. Elizabeth the charmer. Elizabeth the politician. Elizabeth the mother to all. Elizabeth the self-declared virgin. Elizabeth the Queen. Elizabeth the glorious Gloriana. Elizabeth the first and only.
  And now the world and its men and God and his cunning angels place this Stuart before me. This ever-present, ever-lurking, living ghost. She slithers through my brain. Steals into my thoughts like she is slipping into my skin.
  I can predict the actions of a man in power. But I cannot predict those of a woman.
  There is no precedent for the likes of her.
  She invades me.
  She invades me.
  My death is your life. My life is your death.

Silence.

ELIZABETH *signs the warrant.*

Davison!

Beat.

DAVISON *enters.*

DAVISON: Your Majesty?
ELIZABETH: Here.

She hands him the paper.

DAVISON: You signed it.
ELIZABETH: I was asked to sign it, so I signed it. It's just a scrawl on a piece of paper. It doesn't mean much.

DAVISON: But … now that I have received this from you, Your Highness, I must deliver it to the proper authorities.

ELIZABETH: Yes. And?

DAVISON: And once I hand this over, the Queen is dead.

ELIZABETH: I am the Queen.

DAVISON: My apologies. Once I hand this over, Mary Stuart is dead.

ELIZABETH: Mm. Quite a weighty responsibility, wouldn't you agree?

DAVISON *nods.*

It seems it all rests on your shoulders, Davison. A signature is just a signature. But to deliver that signature is a far greater act.
Thank you. Goodbye.

DAVISON *stands stunned, the paper in his hand.*

DAVISON: Your Majesty … I'm not quite sure what I'm supposed / to …

ELIZABETH: I beg your pardon?

DAVISON: I assume that by placing this paper in my hand you do want it delivered?

ELIZABETH: That's entirely up to you.

DAVISON: But, but, but, but—

ELIZABETH: I chose whether to sign or not. Now you can choose whether to deliver or not.

He stares at her, utterly confused.

DAVISON: Your Majesty, I'm not a very smart man—

ELIZABETH: Nonsense. You wouldn't be here if you weren't.

DAVISON: Please tell me plainly what you want me to do with this order.

ELIZABETH: Do what you must do.

DAVISON: So you want the order carried out?

ELIZABETH: Of course I don't. She's a queen.

DAVISON: So you want me to keep it?

ELIZABETH: I can't decide for you.

DAVISON: Yes, you can. You're the Queen.

ELIZABETH: And you're a man. You have free will.

DAVISON: Please, Your Majesty. I need your guidance.

ELIZABETH: Only God can give you guidance. You should ask Him. I am just a woman.

DAVISON: God?

ELIZABETH: God.

DAVISON: In God's name, Queen Elizabeth, please tell me what your order is.

ELIZABETH: Either do your job or don't do it.

DAVISON: I don't know what that ... Here. Take it back.

He tries to hand it back to her.

ELIZABETH: What? No.

DAVISON: Please take it back.

ELIZABETH: You can't leave it with me.

DAVISON: Your Majesty. Gloriana. Please take it.

ELIZABETH: No!

Do your job, man! Whatever that is.

Goodbye.

She leaves.

DAVISON *sits on the floor, stunned.*

BURLEIGH *enters.*

BURLEIGH: What has happened?

DAVISON: I don't want this ... I don't want this ...

BURLEIGH: Did she sign it? Did she sign it, man? Give it to me!

DAVISON: I can't!

BURLEIGH: She has signed Mary Stuart's death warrant?

DAVISON: Yes, but I can't deliver it to you. Her orders were ... confusing ...

BURLEIGH: Give it to me.

DAVISON: No. I can't. Please.

BURLEIGH: Give it to me.

He wrenches it from DAVISON*'s hands and leaves.*

DAVISON: I can't. Please. No. I can't.

END OF ACT FOUR

ACT FIVE

SCENE ONE: MARY

MARY *stands in her space.*

She is a tall, looming figure.

Dressed in a black dress with a white veil that reaches the ground.

She holds her dog.

The GIRL *is nearby.*

PAULET *enters.*

PAULET: Mary.
MARY: Paulet.
PAULET: Can I fetch you anything? Food? A cushion?
MARY: Thank you. No.
PAULET: Perhaps you'd like a book to read? While you wait.
MARY: No.
PAULET: Some paper to write on? Some poetry or final … thoughts?
MARY: No.
PAULET: Some music? Something soft? Calming?
MARY: No.
PAULET: Would you like to rest? Before you …
MARY: No. Last night I slept more soundly than I ever have before.

    Silence.

PAULET: The … event … will take place at eight a.m. tomorrow.
MARY: Thank you.
PAULET: They're just readying things now.
MARY: Thank you.
PAULET: They've got the best man for the job. Which is good.
MARY: Ah.
PAULET: He's a bit nervous. You're his most renowned … So he's a bit
    nervous. Understandably.
MARY: I'm sure he'll do very well.

Silence.

Where is your nephew? Mortimer.

PAULET: He is no longer a member of the court.

MARY: Is he dead?

PAULET: Yes.

MARY: Ah. One more for the blood pit. My condolences to your family, Paulet.

PAULET: Thank you, Mary.

    Silence.

MARY: Has there been any word from my son? The King of Scotland.

PAULET: No.

    Silence.

MARY: Will the Queen be in attendance tomorrow? Will I finally get to meet her?

PAULET: No.

    Silence.

MARY: May I request a priest to hear my final confession?

PAULET: No.

    Beat.

But I can listen. If you like.

MARY: Thank you, my friend. No.

    Silence.

PAULET: I … won't be here tomorrow, Mary.

MARY: Why not?

PAULET: I'll be unemployed. I won't have a prisoner anymore.

MARY: Of course. I'm sorry.

    Beat.

You'll finally get to spend some time with Margaret.

PAULET: And the girls. Yes.

MARY: I'm glad.

PAULET: You have been a most respectable detainee, Mary.

MARY: Thank you, Paulet. You have been a most respectable jailer.

PAULET: It's a pity you two women couldn't have come to some agreement.

MARY: Perhaps if you men made some room in this world, there'd be space for the both of us.

PAULET: Goodbye.

MARY: Goodbye.

He goes to leave, taking her dog with him.

PAULET: You look very striking, Mary.

MARY: Thank you.

PAULET: You're very strong. I couldn't do what you're about to do, Ma'am.

MARY: I know that, sir.

He departs with the dog.

MARY *is left alone.*

She prays.

Au nom du Père et du Fils, et du Saint-Esprit.
My dear Lord.
This cell has been my church for nineteen years. And if you don't mind entering it one last time, I would be most grateful.
This is my last confession. This is my truth.
I stand on the precipice of death and open my conscience to you. I confess.
I confess to a heart filled with envious hate.
I confess to a mind enflamed with vengeful thoughts.
I confess to a life of wild love and sexual abandon.
I confess to mourning my first husband less than I grieved losing the right to his crown.
I confess to hating my Scottish subjects. Lewd, thick-legged, insolent turncoats that they are.
I confess to having my second husband murdered as revenge for the cruelty he inflicted on me daily. He was a cruel, cruel man.
I confess to marrying his killer through fear and reward. He was also a cruel, cruel man.
I confess to being glad when his children bled out of me.
I confess to being an absent mother to my only son.
I confess that the signature on the bottom of every letter that instigated hate against Elizabeth was mine.
I confess to lying about my love for her.

I confess to willing her demise.

I confess to communicating with potential assassins.

I confess to conspiring her death.

I confess to hating her for her actions against me and being struck with jealous awe for her unbreakable will.

I confess to envy. Lust. Covetous thoughts. Pure, boundless, infernal hatred.

And I confess all of this in Your name, Lord.

I committed love for You and I committed hate for You.

I felt all of this for You. I did all of this for You. I am Your warrior. I am Your soldier. I am Your voice. And it won't stop here.

It doesn't matter if I live or die.

Imprisoned, I'm a living saint.

Dead, I'm a martyr.

And who needs Elizabeth's throne when I'll be seated at Your table …?

So …

My Lord.

Soon we meet.

In the end … is my beginning.

She stands. Nods to the GIRL.

The GIRL *places a white veil over* MARY*'s head.*

MARY *stands by the window.*

Lets the crowd outside see her.

SCENE TWO

MARY *is led to the scaffold.*

She removes her white veil to reveal a black dress underneath. Gives the veil to the GIRL.

She removes her black dress to reveal a red dress underneath. Gives the dress to the GIRL.

A man enters in an executioner's mask and stands beside her with an axe.

MARY *lays down. Prone.*

The EXECUTIONER *looks to her. Raises his axe.*

Blackout.

We hear three resonating chops.

Lights up.

The EXECUTIONER *stares into a bucket containing* MARY's *head. Horrified by what he sees.*

SCENE THREE

ELIZABETH, BURLEIGH, SHREWSBURY, LEICESTER, DAVISON.

And the young GIRL.

Mary's blood stains the stage.

ELIZABETH: *I didn't give the order!*

    ELIZABETH *is barefaced, in her robe.*

BURLEIGH: You signed the document, Your Majesty.

ELIZABETH: But I didn't intend for it to be carried out! Not yet!

BURLEIGH: You signed, Gloriana.

ELIZABETH: I thought I'd have more time.

    She turns on DAVISON.

That's not what I instructed you to do.

DAVISON: I don't know what you instructed me to do, Your Majesty.

ELIZABETH: I gave that to you for safekeeping!

DAVISON: You didn't say that, / Your Maj—

ELIZABETH: Are you accusing your queen of wanting her own blood dead?

DAVISON: No, Ma'am! I thought / you—

ELIZABETH: You were supposed to keep it safe, you stupid man! Get out! *Get out!*

    DAVISON *hurries away.*

You have all betrayed my wishes.

BURLEIGH: Your Majesty, you signed the death warrant.

ELIZABETH: It was a ruse! A ploy! Designed to scare her into submission! I was going to show mercy! Of course I was going to give her mercy! She's my cousin! She's practically a sister! Why was it performed with such haste?

BURLEIGH: We had to act, Ma'am. For your own safety. The papists are advancing.

ELIZABETH: But she's a queen! You can't just execute a queen!

BURLEIGH: You just did, / Ma'am.

ELIZABETH: You can't just *execute* a *queen*!

She is furious.

Was it ... swift?

Beat. The men look at one another.

SHREWSBURY: He missed, Ma'am.

ELIZABETH: I don't understand.

BURLEIGH: The executioner ... was nervous.

LEICESTER: The first blow struck her between the shoulder blades. The second didn't sever the head. The executioner used his axe to saw it off.

ELIZABETH: How do you know?

LEICESTER: I was there.

ELIZABETH: Why?

LEICESTER: I wanted to pay my respects.

A lot of people wanted to pay their respects, Bess.

ELIZABETH: There is nothing respectful about watching a woman be publicly mutilated. Why wasn't my mother's executioner called? There should have been no expense spared! I feel sick. I feel sick. Leicester, come here.

LEICESTER *doesn't move.*

My tooth hurts. Come and kiss it better.

LEICESTER *walks away.*

Robert.

Where are you going?

LEICESTER: Home, Your Majesty.

LEICESTER *leaves.*

Silence.

ELIZABETH: Burleigh ...

Her effects. Mary's. Where are they?

BURLEIGH: Burned, Ma'am.

ELIZABETH: All of them? Her poems? Her clothes?

BURLEIGH: We didn't want any of her possessions to end up in the hands of fanatics. They'd turn them into holy relics. Best that we got rid of everything.

ELIZABETH: Did she ... did she write me a letter? She always wrote me letters. She must have written me one more. Surely?

BURLEIGH: No, Your Majesty.

ELIZABETH: Are you sure it's not hidden somewhere? She was very clever like that.

BURLEIGH: I'm sure.

ELIZABETH: Burleigh ...

Has the King of Scotland been informed? Her son.

BURLEIGH: Yes, Your Majesty.

ELIZABETH: What was his response?

BURLEIGH: Nothing. He sends his regards.

She nods.

He goes to leave.

Oh. Your Majesty. Her dog. Shall we have it destroyed?

Beat.

ELIZABETH: No.

BURLEIGH *leaves.*

SHREWSBURY: Your Majesty ...

ELIZABETH: Yes, Shrewsbury?

SHREWSBURY: I'd like to be relieved of the royal seal you have entrusted me with.

ELIZABETH: Why?

SHREWSBURY: I'd like to retire. I'm tired.

ELIZABETH: Retire, you say?

He nods. Waits.

Very well.

SHREWSBURY: Thank you, Queen.

ELIZABETH: Retired. Lucky you. What a luxury.

Thank you for your service, my lord.

SHREWSBURY: You'll reign for a very long time, Elizabeth.

Long live Gloriana.

ELIZABETH: Thank you.

> *He stares at her.*

SHREWSBURY: You look more and more like your father every day.

ELIZABETH: Do I?

> *He goes to leave, then turns.*

SHREWSBURY: Her lips kept moving.

ELIZABETH: What?

SHREWSBURY: Mary Stuart. Her lips. They kept moving for fifteen minutes.

ELIZABETH: What … what was she saying?

SHREWSBURY: She was speaking to God. God let her bodyless head speak for fifteen minutes.

> It was miraculous.

> SHREWSBURY *leaves.*

> ELIZABETH *stands alone.*

SCENE FOUR

ELIZABETH *and the young* GIRL.

ELIZABETH *takes Mary's rosary beads from her gown.*

The GIRL *has a bucket. She sings as she cleans up the blood of Mary.*

ELIZABETH: Hail, holy Queen, Mother of Mercy …

> MARY *appears.*

Our life, our sweetness and our hope.
> To thee do we cry, Poor banished children of Eve …
> To thee do we send up our sighs, mourning and weeping in this valley of tears.

GIRL: [*singing*] Alas, my love, you do me wrong
> To cast me off so discourteously,
> For I have loved you well and long
> Delighting in your company …

MARY: *Salve, Regina, Mater misericordiæ.*
> *Ad te suspiramus, gementes et flentes in hac lacrimarum valle.*
> *Vita, dulcedo, et spes nostra, salve.*
> *Ad te clamamus exsules filii Hevæ …*

ELIZABETH: Turn then, most gracious advocate,
        Thine eyes of mercy toward us …
MARY: *Eia, ergo, advocata nostra,*
        Illos tuos misericordes oculos ad nos converte …
GIRL: [*singing*] Greensleeves was all my joy,
        Greensleeves was my delight,
        Greensleeves was my heart of gold,
        And who but my lady Greensleeves …
ELIZABETH: And after this our exile,
        Show unto us the blessed fruit of thy womb, Jesus.
MARY: *Et Jesum, benedictum fructum ventris tui,*
        Nobis post hoc exsilium ostende.
ELIZABETH: O clement, O loving, O sweet Virgin Mary.
MARY: *O clemens, O pia, O dulcis Virgo Maria.*
ELIZABETH: Queen.
MARY: *Regina.*
ELIZABETH: Queen.
MARY: *Regina.*
ELIZABETH: Forgive us.
MARY: *Propitius esto.*
ELIZABETH and MARY: [*together*] Amen.
GIRL: [*singing*] Still you continue to disdain,
        Enraptured by the fear of me,
        And so, my friends, I still remain
        A woman in captivity …

THE END